Praise for *Searching for My Brothers*

"[Salkin] writes fluidly and crisply throughout.... [He] should appeal not only to many Jewish men—and women—but also to others who seek guidance on becoming a mensch of a man."   —*Kirkus Reviews*

"This important book deals with what it means to be Jewish and male in contemporary Western society.... He ... offers helpful commentary and advice to Jewish men about relationships, ambition, and sexuality.... Unreservedly recommended for all libraries."   —*Library Journal*

"His exploration is thought provoking...."   —*Publishers Weekly*

"Profound and personal, this splendid book will confer blessing on anyone who reads it. *Searching for My Brothers* is Rabbi Salkin's best book yet."
                               —Rabbi Harold Kushner, author of
                               When Bad Things Happen to Good People
                               and *How Good Do We Have to Be?*

"Using his life as text, Jeffrey Salkin, in this very moving book, lets [feminist women] understand what it feels like to be a self-conscious and end-of-the-century Jewish male."   —Susan Weidman Schneider,
                               editor in chief, *Lilith* magazine

"Absorbing, provocative, and deeply moving, *Searching for My Brothers* is a book for women as well as men. Rabbi Salkin makes us think hard about the meaning of masculinity and femininity in Jewish life."
                               —Francine Klagsbrun, author of
                   Jewish Days: A Book of Jewish Life and Culture Around the Year

"At a time when the feminist movement is struggling to reconstruct the idea of the Jewish woman, *Searching for My Brothers* arrives to help Jewish men redefine their own sense of masculinity."
                   —Rabbi Charles Simon, Federation of Jewish Men's Clubs

searching

for my

brothers

Jewish Men in a Gentile World

RABBI JEFFREY K. SALKIN, D.MIN.

A Perigee Book

The checklist on pages 132–133 is used with the permission of
Workaholics Anonymous.

A Perigee Book
Published by The Berkley Publishing Group
A division of Penguin Putnam Inc.
375 Hudson Street
New York, New York 10014

Copyright © 1999 by Jeffrey K. Salkin
Book design by Chris Welch
Cover design by Miguel Santana
Cover photograph © Carlos Gustavo/PNI

Published simultaneously in Canada.

G. P. Putnam's Sons edition: October 1999
First Perigee edition: August 2000

Perigee ISBN: 0-399-52615-3

The Penguin Putnam Inc. World Wide Web site address is
http://www.penguinputnam.com

The Library of Congress has catalogued the G. P. Putnam's Sons edition as follows:

Salkin, Jeffrey K., date.
Searching for my brothers : Jewish men in a gentile world /
by Jeffrey K. Salkin.
p. cm.
Includes bibliographical references and index.
ISBN 0-399-14573-7
1. Jewish men—Religious life. 2. Masculinity—
Religious aspects—Judaism. I. Title.
BM725.S25   1999   99-29410 CIP
296.7´081—dc21

Printed in the United States of America

10 9 8 7 6 5 4 3 2 1

contents

acknowledgments

When I first started thinking about this book, I told a female colleague that I was writing about Judaism and men. Her response was telling: "Isn't that redundant?"

I had to giggle because I knew what she meant. Judaism had always seemed to be about and for men. And yet, just as fish probably lack a word for "water," I had always been struck that no one had ever stopped to think about what Judaism really had to say about men's lives *as men*. Years of hearing Jewish feminists prompted me to wonder aloud: What would happen if men started taking Judaism as seriously as women were now starting to? What would a "feminism for Jewish men" look and feel like?

Hence this book. It is a work that emerges from years of thought and struggle. As the reader will notice, many of the incidents in the pages that follow come out of my own life experience, as both a child and a man. As I approach my forty-fifth year of life, this book has served as a vehicle not only for me to learn and relearn ancient and contemporary text, but to discover how my own life has been a text. My learning on the subject of Jewish manhood has been greatly enhanced by long conversations with my friend and partner in Jewish learning, Joel Grishaver. As I was writing this book, his own book on Jewish gender issues came out, and his wisdom has enriched me. The publication of Daniel Boyarin's scholarly book on Jewish masculinity also coincided with my writing process; several times it struck me how our intellectual paths seemed so parallel.

I am grateful to my editors at Putnam, Jeremy Katz and Hillery Borton. From the moment that Jeremy and I met, there was an instant rapport. We are kindred spirits in so many ways, and his enthusiasm for this project has been unstinting and often contagious. Hillery now knows more about Jews (and Jewish men) than she had ever thought possible. For her clarity of vision and language, I am truly grateful. My agent, Ellen Geiger, was an early fan of my work, lovingly nurturing my growth as a writer and serving as a constant cheerleader for my creativity. Our partnership has been a blessing.

The Brotherhood of my congregation, The Community Synagogue, Port Washington, New York, has been a frequent and enthusiastic audience for many of the ideas in this book. Several of the chapters started as lectures to the Brotherhood, and the men's heartfelt responses helped me realize that this conversation about Jewish manhood needed to be broadened. So, too, the national bodies of the National Federation of Temple Brotherhoods and Federation of Jewish Men's Clubs, both of whom have heard me speak on these issues, and whose professional and lay leaders have been unfailingly supportive of my research and my thinking.

As with all my intellectual endeavors, the leadership of The Community Synagogue has been both supportive and understanding. Together we continue to create a Judaism that will touch both hearts and minds. Rabbi Dan Gropper and Rabbi Carol Goldblatt contributed some of their ideas about narrative and text. My secretary, Valerie Cappello, has helped on some of the more mundane tasks relating to this book (such as occasionally staying late and standing on line at Kinko's). Her help is much appreciated.

My wife, Nina, and my two sons, Samuel and Gabriel, have been helpful and cooperative. One of these days I will finally heed the advice that I have so freely given others: that work and home must achieve some kind of balance.

Finally, I dedicate this book to the most important men in my life. My father, George Salkin, was my earliest teacher about manhood. Among everything else that I could say about him as he approaches his seventy-ninth year, his life has been a singular refutation of the old saw that Jewish men don't know how to fix things. Over the past fifteen years, the second father in my life has been my father-in-law, Mel Rubin. I know now how Moses felt about his own father-in-law, Jethro. Mel is, in many ways, a personal hero to me. Both of my fathers are living examples of how age need not, must not, blunt the spirit.

And to the most important man in my life, my oldest son, Samuel Asher Salkin. Samuel, who entered Jewish manhood on September 4, 1999. Samuel, who is already growing into the kind of person I have dreamed about over the years. He is a rare spirit, a loving, laughing young man, a mensch in training.

And yes, to God—to the eternal *Tattenyu*, that loving parent/father/teacher, who is the ultimate source of all my wisdom and whose presence in my life reminds me that some altars are invisible and yet omnipresent.

Jeffrey Salkin
Port Washington, New York

notes on
religious texts

All biblical translations come from *Tanakh: The Holy Scriptures* (Jewish Publication Society). Quotes from rabbinic literature (Talmud and Midrash) have come from the Soncino editions of the Talmud and Midrash, though I have often taken some liberties in recrafting the language to make it more modern. I have relied heavily upon the CD-ROM versions of both of those classic texts, as well as the CD-ROM version of the Bialik-Ravnitzky *Book of Legends*.

During the week when we read in the Torah:
"When Moses had finished the work, the cloud covered the Tent of
Meeting, and the presence of the Lord filled the Tabernacle."
(Exodus 40:33–34)

1 t has been seven years since my father sold the house on Hay Path Road in Bethpage, New York. The only time I drive by it now is when I want to take a nostalgic shortcut on the way to see friends who live farther out on Long Island. And yet as I pass our old house and see the places where I used to play, it is not only sweetness of memory I encounter. There is bitterness as well. As I drive down the hill where we used to live, I wonder where Andy, Tim, and Tom are nowadays. They were the toughs who lived there when I was a kid. Back in the late 1960s, we called them "hoods." The three of them would conspire with hoods down the road to attack me and throw my bike into the woods and my *Newsday*s into the sewer. Their words still echo in my ears: "Hippie Jew faggot!"

What they were really saying was, "You are the Other. You are a stranger. You are not like us. We like sports and thinking about fast cars. You like music and theater and poetry. We have crew cuts, or greased-back hair; your hair is down to your shoulders. We go to Saint Martin of Tours; you go to Suburban Temple." They were engaging in a dark American tradition. During the 1988 presidential campaign, George Bush accused Michael

Dukakis of being a wimp—and then banished broccoli from the White House menu just to prove that he was a "real man." It is as humorous as the Teutonic body builders, Hans and Franz, laughing at the "girlie men" on the old episodes of *Saturday Night Live.* The message is as American as apple pie: When all else fails, accuse your enemies of lacking masculinity.

When I think back on my experiences as a youth, I find myself wondering, What were my adolescent taunters saying about masculinity? What were they saying about America? And what were they saying about Jews? The American definition of masculinity has classically been: toughness, a preference for solitary action, a lack of emotion, a fondness for sports, a respect for military strength, a disdain for eggheaded intellectualism. The American dialogue on masculinity is peppered with proverbs such as "Take it like a man," "Be a man about it," "What are you, a man or a mouse?"

The late German historian, George Mosse, teaches that every culture defines its own sense of true masculinity, and then uses that definition to portray those who are Other as differently masculine. Throughout history, Judaism has been quietly teaching the world a radically different view of masculinity. In order to understand Judaism's view of masculinity, we would have to return to the very source of Judaism—the Bible itself.

Consider how the stories of sibling rivalry in Genesis convey this different view of masculinity. Whenever there is a pair of brothers—Ishmael and Isaac; Esau and Jacob; Joseph and his brothers—one brother is a hunter or a warrior, and the other is more sedentary and peaceful. One brother uses weapons; the other uses the mind. Each time, the one who uses the mind is the one who wins—and often inherits the covenant. Toughness was for "the nations of the world." The mind and spirit were the tests for Jewish manhood. The seeds had been planted. Jewish masculinity was different.

The defining moment in the history of Jewish masculinity happened after the Romans destroyed Jewish independence in the land of Israel in the year 70 of the Common Era. The Jews lost their homeland. They lost their sacred center and their temple. They lost their sense of power.

In the wake of that disaster, the sages did something brilliant. They knew they had been defeated. They knew they had been subjugated. They said to themselves, "In the Roman world, being a man means defending yourself and your community. We have failed to do that. We must redefine what it means to be a man."

Who was this new Jewish man? The new Jewish man revered *Torah rather than toughness*. In the larger world, macho was the art of brawn. The Jewish critique of macho culture began early. In Roman times, the rabbis forbade Jews from going to the gladiator games because of their violence. Likewise, European men may have engaged in falconry and in hunting, but Jewish law forbade hunting because it involved cruelty to animals and would violate the Jewish dietary laws. In the Jewish world, macho became the art of Torah. This is why Jewish men would pray: "Blessed is God, Who has not made me a woman." If one was not a woman, then one was a man—and a real man had access to Torah. The yeshiva and the synagogue were the places where intense Jewish male bonding happened; remember Isaac Bashevis Singer's book *Yentl*. It was about the intense—even homoerotic—relationship between two men in a yeshiva—or rather, one man and one woman disguised as a man. That may have been why Jewish men did not include women in the minyan. The minyan was the ultimate male bonding. To engage in a text, hearing God speaking, and to pray—speaking to God: That was man's work.

Throughout the life cycle, men celebrated Torah, not *toughness*. When bar mitzvah boys proclaimed, "Today I am a man," they were not making a declaration of puberty. They were saying, "I have read and taught publicly from the Torah. The world of Torah is the world of men. Therefore, I have what it takes to be a man in our culture." When the bridegroom taught Torah to his friends before his wedding, *that*—and not American culture's drunken stag party—was how he showed his manhood.

The second definition of Jewish macho was *ethics*. Western culture said, "Be a man." Jewish culture said, "Be a mensch." When the sage Hillel said, "In a place where there are no men, strive to be a man," he did not mean be a man like a Roman gladiator or like characters played by Sylvester Stallone or Arnold Schwarzenegger or Bruce Willis. By "man," he meant, "Be a person of great moral and spiritual integrity." For that reason, Judaism developed a strict moral and ethical code that demanded that men curb their baser instincts and ascend to something higher.

The third definition of Jewish macho was *access to emotions*. Western culture said, "Take it like a man." Be stoic and brave. Betray no outer feeling. But the Torah contains stories about real men who wept aloud. Jacob cried when he met his beloved Rachel. Joseph cried when he reunited with his brothers. Even Esau, that biblical "Marlboro man," cried when he realized that Jacob had cheated him out of his birthright.

And a fourth way of defining Jewish macho was in its understanding of *male sexuality*. Secular culture said, "Go out and sow your wild oats. Boys will be boys, and men will be men." Judaism demanded sexual restraint outside of marriage. Joseph was praiseworthy because he rejected the advances of Potiphar's wife. "Who is heroic?" the sages asked in *Pirkei Avot*, the ethical maxims of the Mishnah. "The one who conquers his *yetzer*, the one who can control his inclinations, the one who has command over his libido."

A thousand years of ghetto living had sharpened the Jewish brain rather than Jewish brawn. Jewish men exercised their muscles primarily through the carrying of sacred tomes and lifting the Torah scroll after the scriptural reading had been completed in the synagogue worship service. That lack of Jewish muscle had a dark side. Jewish men didn't fight. And rivers of Jewish blood flowed in Eastern Europe. Many American Jews came to America because of a particularly grisly event in Jewish history: the Kishinev pogroms of 1903, which killed forty-nine Jews. The Hebrew poet Hayim Nachman Bialik saw the horrors of Kishinev, and he wrote a famous epic poem about it called "In the City of Slaughter." In that poem, he castigated the passive yeshiva students who could defend neither themselves nor their women. He lamented: "Great is the sorrow, and great is the shame.... The grandsons of the Maccabees—they ran like mice, they hid themselves like bedbugs and died the death of dogs wherever found." Remember that in *Maus* the cartoonist Art Spiegelman portrayed Jewish victims of the Shoah as powerless mice.

Bialik's poem had its desired effect. It galvanized Jewish response. It inspired Jews to defend themselves. It inspired Zionism. Never again would Jewish men be passive. Zionism transformed the image of the Jewish man. Theodor Herzl believed that Jewish men should be involved in the martial arts and in dueling societies. The weak yeshiva boy became the bronzed Ari Ben Canaan of the novel and movie *Exodus*. In a best-selling poster that came out after the Six-Day War—a poster that hung on my wall as a teenager—a Hasidic rabbi emerges from a telephone booth, opening his long black coat to reveal a Superman suit. When Ossie Davis eulogized Malcolm X, he reflected on three centuries of black oppression, homelessness, and victimization, and he proclaimed that "Malcolm was our manhood." For Jews, looking at not three centuries but *twenty* centuries of oppression, homelessness, and victimization, Zionism was to be *their* manhood as well.

Jewish men need a way of talking about being Jewish men parallel to the conversations women have been having for the past twenty-five years about their identities as modern Jewish women. We can thank feminism for teaching us that gender is crucial to identity. In a growing number of synagogues, Jewish women have groups for Rosh Chodesh, the celebration of the new moon, as a forum for developing their spirituality. What do Jewish men have that is still exclusively theirs? In liberal Judaism, the minyan as an all-male preserve is gone—and no one mourns its passing. The *shvitz*, the steam bath, that classic center of Jewish male bonding in immigrant neighborhoods, is gone. The yeshiva world is not our world. Jewish men are in trouble.

Jewish men seem to be fleeing from synagogue life and leadership. For many years, Jewish education has become increasingly feminized, with fewer and fewer men entering that noble and crucial field. As a predominantly upper-middle-class group, many Jewish men hold high-power jobs that require long hours, commuting, and business travel. Some of the most creative, assertive, and dynamic Jewish men simply don't have the time to bring these qualities to the synagogue community. In many synagogues, festival morning services seem to be attended primarily by Jewish women. The new spirituality has barely touched Jewish men; it is often perceived as being a woman's enterprise. Men of all faiths often associate spirituality with so-called feminine characteristics: inwardness, openness, vulnerability, and nurturing. By contrast,

American masculinity connotes independence, industriousness, and competition. Spirituality? Religion? No time, no need, no way.

Men constitute only a tiny percentage of converts to Judaism. In almost twenty years in the rabbinate, I have converted hundreds of women but no more than five men. Every rabbi can testify to the frequent apathy of Jewish men when they join their partners at "Introduction to Judaism" classes as a prelude to conversion. Temple youth groups are increasingly filled with young Jewish women craning their necks and wondering, in the words of one Long Island teen, "Where are all the guys?" Jewish adolescent boys report far less of an investment in their Jewish identity than do Jewish girls of the same age.

Jewish men's organizations need to reimagine and reinvent themselves. Jewish men need something more—more than the occasional breakfast, the occasional speaker, sports night, and blood drives. They might not need to create a Jewish version of the evangelical "Promise Keepers" group. But they *do* need to talk. Jewish men need to discuss what it means to be a Jew and to be a man in our times.

What would Jewish men talk about with one another, if they were honest? What are those issues in men's lives that Judaism could address? In the various chapters that follow, we explore the modern face of Jewish masculinity. In the popular culture of the West, Jewish men have often been portrayed as being something *less* than the masculine ideal. Images of Jewish masculinity were often interwoven with anti-Semitic imagery. We will talk about what that has meant to Jews, and how Judaism has rewritten that masculine ideal. Zionism is not only Jewish nationalism. It is not only the longing for the Land of Israel and for national sovereignty on that land. It is the reclamation of Jewish *manhood* after centuries of emasculation. Judaism has something to say about male sexuality—about how we deal with love, lust, and temptation. We find that conversation in Judaism's teachings about the *yet̲zer ha-ra*, the evil inclination that is within every person. For many men, work and career have become the new "holy of holies." Over time, the fire in the belly seems to increase in heat and intensity. Jewish men—indeed, *all* men—need to talk more about the meaning of ambition. For some men, retirement is tantamount to death. Judaism needs to develop a way of reaching the end of life and looking back on the joys and frustrations of career and family.

Bris, ritual circumcision, is the way that Jewish infant boys enter the Jewish people. How do we respond to critiques of ritual circumcision? What does it really mean in the inner lives of those who participate in that ritual? Bar mitzvah should be more than a party. Maybe it should be more of a tribal initiation. If it is a tribal initiation, then we will have to think about what it means for Jews to be a tribe once again. It would mean that we would have to think about what a modern rite of initiation would look like. We would have to think about bringing our tribal elders back into the precious role of wisdom teachers to young Jewish men. It would mean that we would have to think about what wisdom needs to be imparted to young Jewish men—beyond merely Torah-chanting skills.

In this era of politically correct behavior, everyone, it seems, is hung up on how we talk about—and *to*—God. Referring to God as "Father" or "King" or "He" is no longer "kosher." But the image of God as Father and King is not completely outdated, because being a father and being a son can teach us about our relationships with God. Having a relationship with God can teach us about being fathers and sons as well.

In the book of Genesis, Joseph was lost in the wilderness. He had a mission. His father, Jacob, had sent him to find his brothers and to reconcile with them.

A stranger finds him, wandering. "What are you looking for?" asked the stranger.

"I am searching for my brothers," answered Joseph.

There are many men who are doing precisely that. They are searching for their brothers—for other men with whom to share moments of depth and meaning. Too many men are emotionally wounded and spiritually numb. God did not intend for it to be this way. We can heal those wounds and that numbness. When Joseph finally finds his brothers, they sell him into slavery in Egypt. Many years later, the brothers finally reunite. That reunion will touch something deep and palpable within them. It will lift their souls.

Jewish men need ways to lift their souls, to meet the brothers that they carry within them.

searching for my brothers

A Personal Journey

T he night when I spoke with my cousin Brian, it was like hearing the old voice once again. I had not heard that voice in twenty years, and yet it was remarkably unchanged. Through the awkwardness we spoke with each other, and I offered him condolences on the death of his father, my uncle Herb. To speak to his mother again that night after twenty years was to realize how those years have become frozen in time. Her voice is no longer the voice of the relatively young woman in her sixties. She is now in her early eighties, and there is a frailty and a weakness about her that make me realize the depth of the passage of time. We are all twenty years older now.

When my uncle Herb died last month, a piece of me needed consolation as well. It was not so much for his loss, but rather for what is and what is not, for what was and what might have been. It has been twenty years since the incident that tore our family apart. Brian was the cousin that I was always supposed to be like, the cousin to whom I was always supposed to measure up. My steady Bs on countless report cards could barely match his As, and my parents made no secret about it. I also envied him for his proximity to our grandmother, may her memory now also be a blessing.

My aunt and uncle and cousins lived downstairs from her in Queens, in the house that she and Grandpa, may his memory be a blessing, bought in the 1930s.

My cousin Brian has done very well. He is the executive producer of a major late-night television show. Many nights I struggle to keep my eyes open long enough to catch a glimpse of his name as it rolls by on the closing credits. Just to see his name again, and to imagine how he is doing and what he looks like. To think what it might have been like.

I keep thinking of that moment in the Torah when Jacob sends Joseph out to bring back reports of his brothers—his brothers, who have been allowing their anger against him to fester for so long. Joseph was the favorite son of his father, Jacob—he was the one with the coat of many colors, the one with dreams of grandeur. Jacob could not have stopped himself, even if he had tried. His soul ached for his son. Jacob had himself grown up in a home where parents chose between children.

Joseph is wandering aimlessly in the fields near Shechem.

> A man came upon him wandering in the fields. The man asked him, "What are you looking for?" And he said, "I am searching for my brothers. Could you tell me where they are pasturing?" The man said, "They have gone from here, for I heard them say: 'Let us go to Dothan'" (Genesis 37:15–17).

Some believe that Jacob knew just what he was doing. If he had simply wanted reports about his sons, he could have sent a servant. Jacob sent Joseph not to bring back reports about his brothers, but to make *shalom* with his brothers, to seek healing, to repair their damaged relationship.

Genesis Presents a Familiar Dysfunctional Pattern

It is the eternal pattern of the book of Genesis: damaged, shattered relationships between siblings and within families. You cannot tell the Jewish story without the story of brothers and sisters struggling with each other. Genesis is the story of the eternally dysfunctional family that is the Jewish people.

Abraham has two sons—Ishmael and Isaac. Ishmael is cast out, and becomes the ancestor of the Arab peoples, and Isaac wins the covenant. Isaac has two sons—Esau and Jacob. They wrestle in the womb, and emerge from the womb together, with Jacob holding the heel of his brother. Jacob deceives Esau, not once but twice. Jacob is chosen and Esau is cast out. Esau cries when he learns of his fate, and the rabbis say that the cry of Esau continues to resound in our world. You can hear it anytime you listen for it closely. I have seen captains of industry, men who can stare down any competitor, crumble into tears because of the ruptures in their families. I have seen tough Wall Street lawyers in double-breasted suits shut out of shivas for their parents because of some forgotten snub, and I have seen them shake and grow pale. I have heard in their sobs the very sobs of Esau. I now understand why the rabbis say that the Messiah will not come until the tears of Esau have run dry.

The next generation brings forth Joseph and his brothers. Joseph is cast out, but he is the one who is chosen. When Joseph finds his brothers, their hatred erupts. They strip off his coat of many colors. They throw him into the pit. They sell him into slavery in Egypt. Joseph becomes powerful in Egypt, and in the midst of famine his brothers come down to Egypt, and there they stay, and become slaves. It was all because of the coat. The Midrash, the rabbinic retelling and interpretation of biblical texts, states: **"Because of two yards of colored fabric, we became slaves in Egypt."**

One is chosen, one is cast out. This is the grand drama of Genesis: the battle between brothers. With sisters it is not much different. Rachel and Leah are rivals for the love of Jacob, with Leah using her fertility as an unwitting club in the battle. In every generation, from generation to generation.

The Jewish scholar Yosef Hayim Yerushalmi suggests that the Oedipus complex—the battle between father and son—is not at the heart of civilization. No, Yerushalmi says, it is the Cain complex—the battle between siblings. Yerushalmi notes that the tension between Judaism and Christianity is sibling rivalry—each one battling for the exclusive love of God. In her book *The Curse of Cain*, Regina Schwartz bemoans what she calls the Torah's scarcity principle—this painful idea that there can only be one land, one covenant, one blessing. It is, she suggests, the dark side of monotheism.

What Do I Seek?

Back to the nameless stranger who stops Joseph in the wilderness. "What are you looking for?" he asks. I am searching for what our family used to be.

My cousin and I were born within months of each other. He was the son of my father's sister and her husband. Our childhood was filled with Thanksgiving dinners and Passover seders. It was filled with Sunday afternoons, walking around the block and playing with the other kids. Even then the Jamaica neighborhood was starting to go bad, but Brian knew where it was safe. Seeing him and his family was a double treat, for it allowed us to see Grandma as well. Cousins. Aunts. Uncles. Grandma. Who asks the Four Questions? Who gets the turkey drumstick? It was the way of Jewish family life. It was Barry Levinson's *Avalon*. It was the Jewish version of a Norman Rockwell painting on a *yontif* (holiday) card.

Then came the moment we all dreaded. Grandma was ninety. She had a stroke. She had to go into a nursing home. There was hardly enough money for it, and so the family prepared to sell her house. My aunt and uncle refused to move out. They believed that they deserved to live there forever.

I remember how my father had to take his sister and brother-in-law to court. I remember how upsetting it was to have the case presented before a strange judge, a non-Jewish judge, who could have more easily and economically read a Philip Roth novel in order to get the nuances. There was the decision. Brian's parents—my aunt and uncle—had to move out. The house had to be sold. It was what the family had to do in order to sustain our grandmother.

Then came Thanksgiving weekend, 1978. I was home from rabbinical school that weekend. My father went to do some carpentry work at my grandmother's house. It was strange for him to have tarried so long on the errand. My mother and I wondered about him, and we worried about him. He came home late that evening. When he walked into the house, he had a bruise on his cheek. There had been a fight at the house. My uncle had come after my father with a baseball bat. I will never forget my mother's passionate embrace of my father: "Oh, my God, to think that you could have been killed!" That is one of my most enduring memories of my mother—her girlish passion at that moment.

Our Family Torah

I remembered that moment this past summer. I was thinking of that moment when my brother and sister-in-law and I visited North Adams, Massachusetts. North Adams is a slowly dying manufacturing town on the Vermont border where our family first lived in America. Every Jew in North Adams is our *landsman* (a person from the same community). Every Jew in America should have his or her own private *shtetl*, and North Adams is ours. We drove up there from Stockbridge on a Sabbath morning in July. We found the house where my father and his sisters were born—142 Ashland Street. My father was born on the porch of that house—I suspect because the medical insurance would allow the midwife to come only as far as the porch.

Then we went to the synagogue that my grandfather and great-uncles had helped found. Services were over, and a small group of stalwarts were cleaning up from the kiddush. They took us on a tour of the synagogue and I looked at the memorial plaques in the sanctuary. I knew every name from family folklore—this one a cousin, that one a sort of cousin, and that one a distant maybe relative who married Doris Day and who brought her up to North Adams to meet everyone—and they still talk about it.

One of the older congregants asks again, "Who was your grandfather?"

"Max Salkin," I say.

"Any relation to Louis Salkin?"

"Yes, Louis Salkin was his brother. But we don't talk about him."

Back in 1924, he and Grandpa Max got into a vicious fight over who would run the family dry-goods store. Grandpa lost, and therefore was exiled to Queens. Louis won—and that victory severed his family from ours forever. A few years ago, as I was making a U-turn in Manchester, Vermont, I saw a house with a lawyer's shingle on it with the name Salkin. Perhaps one of Louis's children or grandchildren, I speculated. But the Louis Salkin line has disappeared. They are out of our family memory. The Book of Genesis painstakingly—even lovingly—records the names of the children of Ishmael and the children of Esau. The Jewish mystics said that someday the names of the children of Esau will be revealed to be the most important text in the Torah. But Louis Salkin and his line—they are no longer in our family Torah.

And there you have the pattern of our family. Max severed from Louis over a store. My father severed from his older sister over a house. My brother and I are getting closer all the time, working hard to defeat that old genetic disposition.

The Zohar, the cardinal text of Jewish mysticism, teaches: "Woe to those who think that the Torah is mere stories." The Torah is not mere stories. It is our life. It is the very garment of God. The Torah is like an onion. When you peel back the layers, it makes you cry.

A Family Repair Kit

And so you will ask me, What have you learned from all this? I have learned that the time it took me to dial my cousin's number in California when his father died was the longest five seconds in my life. I have learned that it can take only five seconds to clean up years of emotional detritus. Each time I have done *teshuvah*, repentance, I have learned the great spiritual truth of life. In our time, when everyone is looking for the great inner high, Judaism's great spiritual high is the moment when we let it go. Some say it is an endorphin high. That is a good biochemical understanding of what is going on. But it may be God working within us. It may also be God speaking to us.

The Torah (Leviticus 19:18) commands us not to bear grudges. The anger we choose not to lose becomes the grudge that we carry, and that we guard zealously, and that we place into the *aron ha-kodesh*, the Holy Ark, of our lives, and that we take out from time to time and unroll and from which we can all chant perfectly. The grudge is the poison of our lives. The Jews did not poison the wells of medieval Europe, but we do keep the poison in the wells of our souls, and we let it slosh around, saturating every fiber of our beings. There is an angel of forgetfulness named Purah. A tale is told of a certain rabbi. During his lifetime he remembered everything he had heard or seen. But if someone sinned against him, Purah, the angel of amnesia, would come and place her hands on his head, and he would forget everything bad that had happened to him. Find that angel and make friends with her. Remember all that you must remember and forget all that you must forget. Let go of the named and nameless grudges that you carry with you. Let it go. Let the smallness go. Let the ugliness go. Let it go. Remember the sign at the baggage carousel at LaGuardia Airport: "Check baggage carefully. All bags look alike." Look for a place to check your baggage, and realize that there is some baggage better off left on the circular conveyor belt at the end of the journey.

A story is told of two rabbis who were traveling together. They came upon a young woman who needed help getting across a stream. So one of the rabbis picked her up and carried her across.

Days passed. The other rabbi became curt with him. He wouldn't speak to him. He was rude to him. Finally, the first rabbi—the rabbi who carried the woman—asked his companion, "What's going on? You have been rather short with me lately. Have I done something to offend you?" "Well," the other rabbi said, "it's about that young woman. Rabbis like us, *frumme yidn* [pious Jews]—we shouldn't get that close to women." To which the first rabbi replied: "I put that woman down three days ago. Are you still carrying her?"

Are you still carrying her? Are you still carrying texts within your invisible ark? The Torah is the story of division, the cellular mitosis of the Jewish people. And yet in each generation in Torah, there is reconciliation. Ishmael and Isaac reunite—though it is only at the grave of their father Abraham. Jacob and Esau reunite—and Jacob says that to see his brother is like looking into the very face of God. Joseph and his brothers reunite—with tears and sobs so loud that the noise carries into the very house of Pharaoh. "What are you looking for?" the stranger had asked Joseph. "I am searching for my brothers," he replied. He found them, and he figured out who they really were, years later in Egypt. "I am Joseph!" he cries out to them between choking tears. "Is my father still alive?"

"What are you looking for?" the stranger asked Joseph. "I am searching for my brothers. Do you know where they might be pasturing?" And the mysterious stranger sent him to Dothan. Joseph did not know that he was going there to reconcile with his brothers. It did not work out that way. Not yet, anyway.

As ambivalent as the memory will be, I will remember my uncle Herb on Yom Kippur at the *yizkor* memorial service. He is part of my Torah. I will pray that my grandfather Max Salkin and his brother Louis Salkin are sitting down to tea together in the world to come—and they are saying to each other: "Max, Louis, how could we have let this happen? What will our children say? What will our grandchildren say?"

"Max, Max," Louis will say. "Max, don't worry. Don't you know? Your grandson is now a rabbi somewhere on Long Island. And even now, even now he is teaching the story of what happened to us, and what happened to the siblings in Torah, and he is saying that the sacred scroll can be rewritten."

"it is not good for man to be alone"

What the Bible Teaches
About Masculinity

S everal months ago, I was working with two young boys who were preparing to become *bnei mitzvah* on the same Sabbath morning. These kids were as different as two thirteen-year-old boys could be. One boy was tall, with the physique of a body-builder and the foreshadowing of a beard. His voice had already fully changed. The other boy was thin, smooth-skinned, soft, and docile, his voice still a reedy alto. I was trying to teach them something about Jewish law. In order to do so, I compared the rules of various sports with Jewish teachings. The big boy played basketball and was on his school's wrestling team. The other boy, however, was clueless in that area. "I don't really like sports," he said.

"Well, okay, so what are you into?" I asked.

"Oh, you know—poetry, art, music, hanging out with my friends."

The first thing that went through my mind was: Uh-oh. This kid's got problems. Zane Grey, the western writer, once said, "All boys love baseball. And if they don't like baseball, then they're not real boys." To be a young man in the suburbs means that you have to play a sport. And if you don't . . . well, like I said to myself, uh-oh.

Where did I ever get this idea? Certainly not from *my* life.

I grew up in Bethpage, New York, in the late 1950s and 1960s. Bethpage was a middle-middle-class community, populated by middle managers, smack in the geographic middle of Long Island, in the middle of the century. Like every other suburban kid, I loved baseball. I collected baseball cards. One summer my family visited the Baseball Hall of Fame in Cooperstown, New York. To me, it was like making a pilgrimage to Jerusalem. I played in Little League for two seasons. Despite my passion for baseball, I was never good at it. I could hit pretty well, but I could never quite catch a baseball properly. I remember the coach, a good-natured suburban father like my own dad, working with me patiently, trying to get me to focus on the ball.

Little League was ultimately a washout. The coach convinced me to leave the team. The day I turned in my uniform was one of the most painful days in my childhood. It was an admission of defeat, the realization that I would never be like the other boys. As a consolation prize, my dad drove me to the bookstore at the mall and let me buy a book.

By the time I was thirteen, I was already over six feet tall. My total lack of coordination put a damper on any basketball coach's fantasies. To this day, children and adults alike ask me if I played basketball. I joke that I won the first-ever "Anti-Basketball Scholarship" in high school, in which I received massive amounts of money in exchange for my solemn commitment *never* to play basketball.

In high school, I hated physical education classes. The truth is, I was afraid of the gym teachers. They were recently discharged veterans who had fond memories of military service. This must have been what inspired them to run gym class as they would a Marine battalion. They once urged some jocks to submit a weaker kid to "group therapy." This meant that they beat him up in the locker room. The locker room was a dark territory, neither hallway nor classroom, a place with no rules, a place where anything could happen. To make matters worse for me, the gym teachers at our high school were not exactly candidates for the Anti-Defamation League awards dinner. I remember a football coach yelling at Charlie Cohen: "If you wanna make the team, Cohen, you better change your name."

So I forgot about sports. I developed other talents and interests: reading, music, and theater. Those arenas were no less competitive than the sports field. As one burly high school athlete once told me, "Face it, Salkin, you're a drama jock." I would never attract girls because of my athletic ability. So I figured out how to use sensitivity as seduction: reading them poetry or singing songs I had written. It frequently worked.

When I was in my twenties, I discovered why I wasn't athletic. I learned that I had a congenital eye-muscle problem that caused me to see double. That explained why I could never quite catch a ball correctly. By then, it did not matter. The jeers on the playing fields still echoed in my ears. It is very tough to be a sissy in suburbia.

It is thirty years later. My oldest boy, Samuel, was also born with a congenital eye problem. He lacks a lens in one eye, which makes one of his eyes green and the other brown. "Tell the girls that you have magic eyes," I kid him. He laughs. Years ago, when I watched him try to play soccer and basketball, it was painful. He was always the only Jewish kid on his team. The gentile boys in our community were much better athletes.

Two days ago Sam had his moment of truth in Little League. He hit a line-drive single, driving home two kids on base, breaking a tie, and single-handedly winning the game for his team. I wept with joy for his victory. Had he redeemed me from my own athletic failures?

Tales of Two Brothers

The two boys in my study represented two competing visions of masculinity. They were the Torah of Jewish manhood. The great narrative code of the book of Genesis is sibling rivalry. How does this rivalry play out? One brother is always tough and classically masculine, and the other brother is softer and intellectual. Only one brother can win the covenant. The winner is always the weaker son. The stronger brother becomes something else, someone else, someone Other.

That's who *we* were as well, we Jews—the younger, weaker brother among the nations. But our weakness was somewhat holy. And so we might ask: What does it mean to be a man in the Torah?

ISAAC AND ISHMAEL

When the first Jews, Abram and Sarai, whose names will be changed to Abraham and Sarah, could not have children, Sarai offered her Egyptian handmaiden, Hagar, to Abram for childbearing. As soon as Hagar became pregnant, her continued presence in Abram's household became unbearable to Sarai. And so Abram gave Sarai total power over the visibly pregnant Hagar. "Do with her what you want," he says. And so Sarai treated her miserably, and Hagar fled into the wilderness. There an angel told her that she was pregnant with a child whose name would be Ishmael. **"He will be a wild ass of a man; his hand against everyone, and everyone's hand against him; he shall dwell alongside of all his kinsmen" (Genesis 16:12).** Sometime later, despite her being well advanced in years, Sarah bore a child—Isaac, "the one who causes laughter." Abraham made a great feast on the day that Isaac was weaned. Sarah noticed that Ishmael, who was already thirteen years old, was *metzachek*—a problematic word. The word comes from the Hebrew root *tzachak*, meaning "to laugh," the same root as is found in Isaac's Hebrew name, Yitzchak. Is it, as Norman Cohen, professor of Midrash at Hebrew Union College–Jewish Institute of Religion, has suggested, that Sarah notices that Ishmael resembles Isaac more than she would have liked to admit, even to herself?

What was Ishmael doing? There are many possible translations of *metzachek*. Was Ishmael *playing?* Or *mocking* the feast? Or *mocking* Isaac? And if so, who could really blame him? Imagine how he must have felt—his presence in the household barely acknowledged, and his younger brother the source of such joy!

Whatever his minor crime might have been, Ishmael and his mother Hagar could not stay in Abraham and Sarah's household. **"She said to Abraham, 'Cast out that slave woman and her son, for the son of that slave shall not share in the inheritance with my son, Isaac"** (Genesis 21:10). Hagar and Ishmael are unnamed in the text; they are simply the help and her kid. Again, Abraham consented to Sarah's cruelty. Abraham cast the hapless pair out into the wilderness. There a spring of water miraculously welled up in the desert and revived the almost-dying Ishmael. An angel reassured Hagar that her son would grow up to become a great nation—indeed, Ishmael is considered the ancestor of the Arabs. **"God was with the boy and he grew up; he dwelt in the wilderness, and became a bowman. He lived in the wilderness of Paran; and his mother got a wife for him from the land of Egypt"** (Genesis 21:20–21).

Who is Ishmael? He is described as a *pere adam*, a "wild ass of a man." Ishmael is less than fully human; he is like a boy reared by wolves in the wilderness. He is destined to be violent, confrontational, an archer, a warrior, a loner. He will dwell *al penei kol echav*, "alongside of all his kinsmen." But the phrase *al penei* also can be translated as "in the face of." Ishmael will get into people's faces, which is precisely what gets him and his mother thrown out of Abraham and Sarah's household. Ishmael is the one who *metzachek*/laughs on the sidelines. Yet Isaac/*Yitzchak* bears the name "laughter." Perhaps Ishmael's laughter reminds Sarah of her earlier infertility. Perhaps it was precisely because of what he was doing— standing on the sidelines, poking fun and mocking the festivities.

The ancient rabbis who interpreted the Torah have a field day with that tricky Hebrew word *metzachek*. What was Ishmael really doing? The rabbis imagined that Ishmael committed every classic sin. Maybe Ishmael was "fooling around" violently. One midrash (rabbinic intepretation) portrays Ishmael as shooting arrows at Isaac, claiming to be "fooling around" (*Genesis Rabbah* 53:11). The midrash foresees that he will become a highwayman and a robber. Ishmael will use his archery skills to hunt defenseless animals (*Genesis Rabbah* 49:5). Maybe Ishmael was "fooling around" sexually. The midrashim suggest that he is polymorphously perverse—sexually violating both married women *and* Isaac. Maybe Ishmael was "fooling around" religiously by worshiping idols. A midrash suggests that Ishmael used to catch locusts and sacrifice them to idols as "make-believe sacrifices" (*Genesis Rabbah* 53:11). Ishmael is like the wilderness, which is his home. He is open to everything—a man with no boundaries, a man untouched by civilization.

The ancient rabbis make a lot out of the fact that Ishmael was circumcised when he was thirteen years old (Genesis 17:25), as opposed to his brother Isaac, who was circumcised when he was eight days old (Genesis 21:4). In one midrash, Ishmael brags about this to his brother. He can take the pain; he is a "real man." Isaac, not to be undone, laughs at Ishmael. "Big deal!" he retorts. "That was just a little piece of flesh. There will come a time when

God will tell my father Abraham to sacrifice me, and I will not even resist." Circumcision at thirteen is nothing. Isaac is so macho that he is willing to sacrifice himself to God.

And yet who is Isaac? Someone once said that there is substantial proof that Isaac really lived: No nation would invent an ancestor like him. No nation, except the Jews.

In contrast to Ishmael, Isaac is docile and meek. If Ishmael is a man of the wilderness, Isaac is the one who stays at home. That is, until the moment when God tells his father to take him to Mount Moriah and offer him as a sacrifice there. The story of the Akedah, the binding, is arguably the most powerful and best-known story in the entire Jewish Bible. It looms large within the Jewish consciousness. This is primarily because Jews hear the story in synagogue on Rosh Hashanah, the Jewish New Year, which is theological prime time.

Is something wrong with Isaac? When God tells Abraham to take Isaac to Moriah, Isaac shows no sign of resistance, even though, according to one interpretation, he must have been thirty-seven years old at the time. Is this son of a menopausal woman mentally retarded? There is a whole strand of the rabbinic tradition that sees Isaac as a willing sacrifice. Isaac is powerless at the Akedah. He is either unable or unwilling to resist. In several legends, Isaac actually dies on Mount Moriah, and then comes back to life. The rabbis told those tales in the wake of the destruction of Judean independence, after the Romans destroyed the Temple in Jerusalem in 70 C.E. For Jews living in exile and in subjugation, Isaac symbolized their plight, and served as a model for their faith. He accepted what befell him with perfect faith. He became, therefore, the classic Jewish man—*passive*. His blindness in old age is even part of his passivity. One midrash says that the angels wept when they saw Isaac on the altar. Their tears fell into his eyes, and he was blinded forever. Centuries later, Isaac would become the most popular name for Jewish boys in medieval Europe, for each parent imagined that their child might, in fact, become a ghastly sacrifice, slaughtered on the pyres of marauding enemies.

WHOSE PROBLEM IS BARRENNESS?

Years later, Isaac would take Rebecca as his wife. Actually, this is a bit of an overstatement. Isaac does not choose Rebecca. Abraham's servant, Eliezer, chooses her for him. Was Isaac too weak to make the long journey back to the old family homestead, where Rebecca would be found?

Like Abraham and Sarah, Isaac and Rebecca are childless. Whose problem is it? Just Rebecca's, and not Isaac's? One passage in the Talmud (*Yevamot* 64a–b) suggests that even though Rebecca was barren, Isaac was also sterile. The rabbis create an image: Isaac and Rebecca, unified in their pain and in their shame, at opposite sides of the tent, both praying to God in their solitude.

I know how Isaac felt.

"So," strangers ask, "why do you have one son who is twelve and one who is six?"

We didn't plan on it that way. Our older boy, Samuel, was effortless. We weren't even trying. But we had to endure six long years of secondary infertility before his brother Gabriel came. And those years taught me a lot of Torah.

Like Isaac in his solitude, I prayed. We could hardly bear to be around pregnant women or families with newborns. Well-meaning people would say, "Have fun trying." Sex on demand is not fun. It reduces you to being a baby machine, or a sperm count with legs. Forget about being in the mood. There were several miscarriages. One year, there was a miscarriage on the day before

Rosh Hashanah. We will never forget that Rosh Hashanah. To hear the story of the Akedah, the binding of Isaac—the near-sacrifice of a long-awaited son—seemed to mock our pain. With every failed pregnancy, we believed that we were climbing modern versions of Mount Moriah, and that we were seeing our hopes and our future mocked. We would hear the sounds of the shofar, and we would imagine the blasts as cries of a newborn. We would hear the words of the liturgy—"Today is the birthday of the world"—and long to be planning a bris or a baby-naming for a girl.

Sometimes Nina and I said to each other: "Look, maybe this is it. Maybe we'll just have one child. People do, and they are happy, and they are fulfilled." But we knew something else. For Jews, childbirth is not simply baby-hunger. It is eternity hunger. After we died, we wanted there to be two more Jews to take our places. How would Sam spend the Jewish holidays after we were gone? What would he do? With whom would he have dinner? We could not tolerate the possibility that he would be alone.

Nina became an activist for the infertile, becoming involved in support groups and their various networks of lives and stories. We went through aggressive medical intervention. All along I assumed that it was Nina's problem. It was, but only partially. It was mine as well. Like Isaac and Rebecca, we shared the problem. I went under the knife. I limped out of the short procedure unit at Long Island Jewish Hospital. It was a heroic limp—like the limp of my biblical namesake Jacob. The result of that surgery is now seven years old. His name is Gabriel.

Did the Akedah traumatize Isaac? Did that trauma cause him to become merely passive, a pale reflection of his father? Both Abraham and Isaac have barren wives. Both Abraham and Isaac try to deceive Philistine kings into thinking that their wives are their sisters, ostensibly for monetary gain. Abraham dug wells; Isaac redug the same wells. Abraham sent a son out into the wilderness, bereft of the covenant. So did Isaac. This is one of those things that men worry about: Is my life my own? Am I simply repeating the patterns of my father? How well I remember the first time I yelled at my son about his homework. I stopped myself in midsentence: "Wait a second. Where did I hear that voice before?" My lips were saying the words, but I was hearing my father's voice. The sons of powerful fathers live with the nagging question: "Will I ever be able to live up to my father's example?" In fact, psychiatrists call this "the Isaac syndrome."

JACOB AND ESAU

When Isaac and Rebecca's sons are born, it is only after deep struggle and pain. Even in infancy, the lads struggled together within her, prompting Rebecca to ask God the first existential question in history: "If this is so, why do I exist?" She exists, says God, because there are two nations within her. There were not only two nations, but also two different ways of looking at the world. There were two different kinds of men, and two different kinds of maleness.

Jacob is a dweller in tents. He is the inner man, the private man. When he wrestles with the nameless stranger at the banks of the Jabbok, he is wounded in his *yerech*—in his groin, in his masculinity. Jacob becomes the wounded healer of mythology, the paradoxical hero who limps into the sunrise as opposed to the Western hero, who gallops off into the sunset. Abram becomes Abraham when he is circumcised. Jacob becomes Yisrael when he is wounded in his own virility.

Esau is as close as Torah gets to Robert Bly's *Iron John*. Esau is hairy, which is an almost universal sign of the primitive man. Esau is a hunter, which is one reason why Jews classically don't hunt. Esau brought the hunted animals to Jacob, who would prepare them as food for Isaac. Ishmael is "a wild ass of a man," and there is something animal-like in Esau as well. In one pivotal scene, he comes home to Jacob, famished from the hunt. Jacob forces him to sell his birthright as the older son in exchange for a bowl of soup. When Esau devours the soup, he does so as an animal. The medieval French commentator Rashi connects the name Esau with the Hebrew term *asah*, "to make." Esau comes into this world fully made. He is born with hair, beard, and teeth. With Esau, what you see is what you get. He will not grow. He cannot grow. Rashi puts it this way: Esau is *batel*, vacant. He is a hunter because he is searching for some kind of organizing principle in his life.

Where is Esau's place? It is the field. But the rabbis said that the field in which he wandered was, in fact, Mount Moriah, the site in ancient Jerusalem where his father Isaac had been offered as an almost-sacrifice. Centuries later, the Temple would be built on that site.

I imagine Esau walking back to Moriah, kicking over the large stones with his foot, wondering which of them were the stones of the altar upon which his father had been bound. "Oh, Father," he says to himself. "Father, once there was a time when Grandfather tied you up here, and scared you half to death. You swore to yourself that you would never be like him. And yet that is exactly how you turned out—just like him.

"And now you lie in bed, blind. The women laugh and say that it all started when Grandpa took you here. They cackle and tell the story about how the angels saw what was happening, and wept, and their tears fell into your eyes, and it was then that your eyesight began to fail.

"Oh, Father, I stand in this place. In days to come, they say that it will be a holy place, the place to which the children of Israel will bring their sacrificial offerings. On this site, they will build their Temple. This is the place where you lay powerless. I swear you must have looked into the eyes of your God, who demanded your passivity.

"In this place, I swear: I will never be that way. Never. Never."

No—Esau is tough, a hunter, murderous. The struggle between Jacob and Esau began in the womb, though the midrash tells us that "barely a membrane separated them," i.e., we are always more like the Other than we think. The Midrash teaches that the physical and spiritual separation between Jacob and Esau began at the age of thirteen. At that age, Jacob and Esau went their own ways. Jacob went to learn about the ways of God. Esau went to the worship of idols. One became the good boy, the *nachas*-producer; the other rebelled.

Esau hated Jacob for cheating him—not once, but twice. The first time, Jacob cheated Esau out of the birthright due him as the oldest son. The second time, Jacob tricked his blind father, Isaac, into giving him the blessing intended for Esau.

The Talmud teaches that Esau restrained the evil within him until the day his grandfather Abraham died. Abraham's death liberated Esau from the strangling chains of the pretension of civilization. On the day of Abraham's death, says the Talmud (*Baba Batra* 6b), Esau raped a maiden, murdered a man, and denied that there was a God. Years later, Esau and Jacob reunite. The Bible will state that Esau kisses Jacob's neck (Genesis 33:4). But the true translation of *vayichabkehu*, "he kissed him," is ambiguous. It might also mean that Esau *bit* him. He is, after all, a redhead, as vampires are frequently portrayed in folklore. The Midrash

(*Pirkei deRebbe Eliezer* 36) imagines Esau saying: "I will not kill my brother with bow and arrow, but I will suck his blood with my mouth."

THE SECRET OF ISAAC'S LOVE

Why did Isaac love Esau so much? "Isaac favored Esau because he had a taste for game." Isaac's love for Esau was based on what Esau was capable of doing for him. Isaac loved venison. Isaac loved Esau because he loved the food that Esau would bring him. It was, so the sages might say, an *ahavah she-teluyah ba-davar,* a love that was dependent upon the fulfillment of some ulterior motive.

Isaac loved Esau because he reminded him of something deep and unnamed. He would look at Esau coming in from the hunt and would feel the hurt inside. He could not name the hurt. He could not name the wound.

But this he knew, and this he sensed. His son Esau was a hairy man. He was a hunter. He carried a bow and arrow with him wherever he went. He was inarticulate. He was a rebellious lad whose future already seemed murky.

Where, Isaac asked himself constantly, where had he seen this lad before? Who was this young man whose life was so different from that of his brother? It was only on his deathbed that he finally knew. It was only then that he understood his profound love for this wild, violent, impetuous son who had been such a disappointment in everyone's eyes, this son who was a skillful hunter, this son who was a man of the bow. Isaac suddenly remembered, and his eyes—eyes which had long ago become blind—filled with tears.

Esau was Ishmael, Isaac's half brother. Esau was Ishmael, the son that Abraham had had with the Egyptian handmaiden Hagar. Esau was Ishmael, the son who was cast out into the wilderness with his mother. He was the son who almost died in the desert. He was the wild, violent, impetuous son who became an expert bowman and became the father of a great nation. Isaac suddenly remembered and ached for his brother. Even across the sands and even across the years, Isaac felt the love for his brother.

At that moment Isaac knew that he did not love Esau only because he loved the venison Esau brought him. Isaac loved Esau because Esau brought something to him that he missed deeply and craved immeasurably. He loved Esau because Esau reminded him of the piece of himself that had been torn from him years ago in the wilderness. He missed that piece of himself and mourned for it. It was the missing piece of his soul.

"Have you no blessing for me, Father?" Esau asked. He wept aloud.

Isaac pulled a broken piece of matzah, unleavened bread, from beneath his robe, and handed it to his son Esau.

"What is that, Father?" Esau asked.

"It is the afikomen, my son."

"What is an afikomen?" Esau asked.

"There will come a time, my son, when Jacob's descendants will be slaves in Egypt. They will go free. And every year, they will eat a dinner—a Passover seder—and they will tell the story of their enslavement, and how they got out, and how God redeemed them. They will eat matzah to remind them of their suffering. They will break a piece of matzah at the beginning of the Passover seder, and they will hide it, and only after it is found can the seder continue."

Esau handled the matzah gingerly. He fingered its jagged edges, felt its harshness, its brokenness.

"Why do you hand this to me, Father? I asked for a blessing, and you gave me a piece of broken matzah?"

Jacob sighed. "Ah, my son, I give it to you so that you will know that this is the way of the world. This is the way of brothers. The jaggedness of the matzah is the jagged edge of the reality of this world. There is brokenness, and there will always be brokenness, until the end of days. Learn to know it. Learn to bless it, if you can."

That is why one of Esau's wives is Machalat, the daughter of Ishmael. There he found his past. There he embraced a daughter of the man who was his mirror image: the young lad who had been a refugee of the covenant . . . the man who had come to know the wilderness . . . the man who had come to know the bow . . . the man who had become a hunter. Some say that when Esau married Machalat he fell on his uncle Ishmael and wept with grief and joy. He had found a part of himself that he had never known—the uncle who was just like him. He had found the missing piece of his soul. There are those who say that when Esau left Isaac, the old man wept with joy and grief. Grief that he had lost the son who reminded him of Ishmael. Joy that he had discovered the piece of himself that he had once thought was gone. He had found the missing piece of his soul.

JOSEPH AND HIS BROTHERS

From Jacob and Esau, we journey to the next generation, to Joseph and his brothers. Joseph is the second youngest of Jacob's children. He is the son of the beloved Rachel, who dies while giving birth to his younger brother, Benjamin. Jacob dotes upon

Joseph, giving him a coat of many colors, favoring him over all his brothers. Joseph is a dreamer and an interpreter of dreams. He demonstrates the classic Jewish survival skills of the Diaspora— dream interpretation and management. He uses his Jewish smarts to get ahead in Egypt, assume power, and restructure the Egyptian economy. He has the uniquely Jewish Diaspora macho of Henry Kissinger. But Joseph is also the most effeminized man in Genesis. Consider, first, the clothing that he wears.

The Hebrew term for Joseph's coat is *ketonet passim*. It is not the only *ketonet passim* in the Bible. II Samuel 13 tells the graphic story of King David's son Amnon and his incestuous lust for his half sister Tamar. Amnon rapes Tamar, and then, in postcoital disgust, sends her away. Like Joseph, she wore a *ketonet passim*, **"for maiden princesses were customarily dressed in such garments."** So Joseph is more than effeminized; he is wearing female garments. Joseph is the virginal "daughter" "raped" by his half brothers.

The Midrash describes Joseph as a dandy who bedaubed his eyes and slicked back his hair and walked with a mincing step. He gossiped about his brothers to his father, and ancient Judaism saw gossip as a unique kind of women's discourse. The Midrash says that Joseph accused his brothers of flirting with Canaanite women. When he goes looking for them, he ultimately finds them in Dothan. A modern interpretation suggests that there they were trafficking with the prostitutes who must have been plentiful at that ancient intersection of caravan routes.

By contrast, Joseph's brothers are tougher. Consider their moral résumé. In Genesis 34, Dinah, the daughter of Leah and Jacob, goes out and is seduced by Shechem, a prince of the Hivites, a Canaanite nation. Shechem claims to love her and wants to marry her. The

Shechemites, under the leadership of Shechem's father, Hamor, readily see the economic advantages to intermarrying with the Hebrews. After some negotiation, Dinah's brothers agree to allow the marriage to take place. But there is one condition: the men of Shechem must circumcise themselves. They agree to this, and on the third day, while they are still in pain from the surgery, Dinah's brothers, led by Simeon and Levi, slaughter the people of Shechem. They not only commit a grievous moral sin by reneging on their agreement, they take advantage of the Shechemites when they are in pain.

Finally on his deathbed, Jacob does criticize this transgression (Genesis 49:5–6). He aims his rebuke at Simeon and Levi, who organized the retaliatory strike against Shechem.

Simeon and Levi are a pair; their weapons are tools of lawlessness. Let not my person be included in their council, let not my being be counted in their assembly. For when angry they slay men, and when pleased they maim oxen.

The Midrash (*Genesis Rabbah* 98:5) amplifies Jacob's condemnation. "Those weapons that were in your hands were stolen," the sages imagine Jacob saying. "They belong to Esau, who sold his birthright." The brothers have behaved like Esau. When Joseph tests his brothers in Egypt by imprisoning Simeon and calling for Benjamin to be brought down as a hostage, the Midrash imagines the brothers going on a superhuman rampage. It imagines that Judah threatened to destroy the whole land. The yells of the brothers were so intense that they destroyed the cities of Pithom and Raamses, which remained in ruins for generations until the enslaved Israelites rebuilt them. Their toughness served no purpose; it was macho bravado that was ultimately destructive.

REUNIONS

The more docile brother always inherits the covenant. And yet, he must reunite with his tougher brother or brothers. That is not only how the story moves forward. It is also how the brothers become whole.

Ishmael and Isaac finally reunite. The scene is Abraham's funeral at the Cave of Machpelah in Hebron (Genesis 25:9). I imagine the awkward silence. It is the ancestor of the awkward silences that I have heard at funerals for families marred by infighting. The sixty-something brothers sit in the waiting room at the local Jewish funeral home, each one shooting the other hidden glances. The tension is thick; the two brothers have not spoken in years. It's an old story—a battle over money, or an old inheritance, or an imagined snub. Whatever the reason is, one of the brothers gets up and shuffles over to the other. "Morty, Morty," he says through tears, "let's cut it out, for cryin' out loud. It's time to bury Dad." They embrace and the funeral is ready to begin.

How distant was Isaac from Ishmael? Geographically, not distant at all. Isaac settled in Beer-lahai-roi, the place to which Hagar had fled when she was pregnant with Ishmael. Norman Cohen hints that Isaac went there hoping to find Ishmael. A midrash (Jubilees 2:1–3) suggests that there was a rapprochement between them. They are far more similar than they would like to admit. Ishmael may have laughed because a servant had to go and find a wife for Isaac. That is, until he remembered that his own mother, Hagar, got him a bride from Egypt. Of all the seventy nations that God created, only two will bear the Divine Name *el*—Yisrael and Yishmael.

Jacob and Esau also reunite. The scene is no less tender

than that of Ishmael and Isaac's reunion. It happens after Jacob's wrestling match with the mysterious stranger at the banks of the Jabbok River. Jacob had been wounded in that battle. The next morning, he meets Esau, who has come with a retinue of four hundred men. Jacob is terrified. But the two men fall on each other's neck, weeping—Esau kissing his brother, Jacob saying that seeing Esau's face is like seeing the face of God. Esau invited Jacob to come with him to Seir, but Jacob makes the excuse that the family is too delicate and tired for the journey. He tells his brother, in essence, that he will come visit him soon. "Let's do lunch sometime. I'll call you." And yet the Torah never records their seeing each other again.

Joseph must also find his brothers in order to become whole. "Go see how the flocks are pasturing at Shechem," Jacob had said. And so Joseph went on a journey that turned out to be much longer than the one he had first imagined. A certain nameless man finds Joseph wandering in the wilderness— a foreshadowing, perhaps, of his descendants' forty-year trek through a similar wilderness. "What are you looking for?" asked the stranger. "I am looking for my brothers," Joseph replied. And when he found them, he was sold into slavery.

Joseph *really* finds his brothers many years later in Egypt. The years have changed Joseph from the bratty kid who reported his grandiose dreams to all who would listen into an administrator in Egypt, second in power only to Pharaoh himself. Joseph finally revealed himself to his brothers after he had tested them—tested their loyalty to their weaker brothers, tested them to see if they had truly repented. That reunion was accompanied by loud weeping.

The Bible's Sensitive Men

What is the message that young boys hear in our culture? Finish the sentence: "Big boys don't _____." Right. *Cry*. Men are not supposed to show emotion, or be vulnerable, or talk too much, or be too open. But Jewish men *do* cry—at least Jewish men in the Bible.

Real patriarchs cry. They cry at moments of loss. Abraham cries at the death of Sarah. Jacob cries when he meets Rachel. Jacob cries when he thinks that Joseph is lost. David weeps at the loss of his sons. Men cry out of pain. Ishmael cried when he was in need. The Midrash states (*Genesis Rabbah* 53) that because Ishmael cried, generations later God would cause Miriam's well to spring up and nourish the Jewish people in the wilderness. A man's weeping brings a well of redemptive water in the wilderness.

Biblical men cry when they encounter ethical wrongdoing. When Jacob deceives Esau, he cries with a loud wail. Centuries later, the Jews in Persia would weep over their imminent destruction by the wicked Haman, a descendant of Esau through the line of Amalek. The cries of the Jews in Shushan, the Persian capital, were an echo of Esau's cries.

Men cry when they encounter the past they thought they had lost. When Joseph could no longer hide his identity from his brothers in Egypt, he wept profusely. Men weep when they encounter their own mortality. The Judean king Hezekiah weeps out of fear of his own death (II Kings 20:1–3).

MASCULINE PRIVILEGE

We go from weeping men to a complete reimagination of manhood. Biblical law transforms the image of what it means to be a man. This happens especially in the realm where manhood could be its most destructive—the way wars are fought. On the one hand, the Torah does not condemn war. The Israelites could show no mercy to the seven idolatrous nations of Canaan. They were to be utterly exterminated. On the other hand, there is also ambivalence toward war.

Consider the Israelite code of war as outlined in Deuteronomy 20. The battle begins with a pep talk by a priest, reminding the soldiers that in reality it is God who does the fighting, thus sanctifying the war. The priest immediately makes allowances for those exempt from battle: men who have not yet dedicated homes, or harvested a vineyard, or who are betrothed yet have not been married. Even one who is afraid and disheartened is exempt, because that person would become a threat to morale. For its time, the code of war is a remarkable realization of the real emotional packaging of men.

ETHNIC CLEANSING, BIBLE STYLE?

What about women in war? As the century draws to a close, rape in warfare is back in style. It is a grisly throwback to ancient, unenlightened times. The map of shame is by now well known: Bosnia, where Serbian soldiers rape Muslim women as part of a plan for "ethnic cleansing"; Rwanda, where Hutu troops rape Tutsi women; Algeria, where Islamic rebels kidnap secular women and force them into sexual slavery; Indonesia, where security forces raped ethnic Chinese women.

Recall the movie *Casualties of War,* about a platoon of American soldiers in Vietnam who rape and kill a young Vietnamese woman. In one scene, a rapacious soldier muses aloud, "This is how it's always been. Ever since Genghis Khan, soldiers have been doing this." He was merely participating in a time-honored and glorious tradition. However, one soldier refuses to participate. His comrades suspect that he is homosexual (the fact that he has a wife back home in Minnesota never enters the conversation). But the soldier is a religious man—a Lutheran with no compunctions about speaking to the military chaplain. We can't do this horrible thing, he surmises, because there is something bigger than we.

Judaism would agree. About such wartime atrocities, Judaism would respond with a loud voice: "*Past nicht.* Oh, no, you don't." A tradition that teaches about the kashruth of eating and of sexuality, a tradition that sees its role as the taming influence over human impulse, could scarcely countenance this. There is a kashruth of war as well.

Deuteronomy 21:11–14 reads:

> . . . and if you see among the captives a beautiful woman, and desire her, and you would take her to wife; you shall bring her into your house; and she shall trim her hair, pare her nails, and discard her captive's garb. She shall spend a month's time in your house lamenting her father and mother; after that you may come to her and possess her, and she shall be your wife. Then, should you no longer want her, you must release her outright. You must not sell her for money; since you had your will of her, you must not enslave her.

The Torah commands Israelite soldiers to treat women captives of war graciously and with equity. At a certain point, the soldier either had to marry her (and, said Samson Raphael Hirsch, the nineteenth-century German Orthodox sage, convert her to Judaism) or set her free. Biblical culture slowly began to transform the culture of the ancient Middle East. Power would not be sufficient for the spiritual tasks of life. When the ancient desert tabernacle is built, it is the result of a partnership between Bezalel of the tribe of Judah, the strongest of the tribes, and Oholiab of the tribe of Dan, the weakest of the tribes. The place where Jews meet God represents the intersection of human strength and frailty.

For every biblical hero who is known for his physical strength, we learn that brute power alone is insufficient. The Israelite tribal leader Samson is known for his great strength. But his strength ultimately proves to be blind and suicidal. King David is known for his womanizing and his military victories. Yet he cannot build the first Temple in Jerusalem because his hands are too stained with blood. He is revered more for the authorship of the Psalms than for his competence in battle. The prophet Zechariah will invoke the words of God: "Not by military might and not by power, but by God's spirit." Not by the *sword*, but by *words*.

Jethro, A Male Role Model

Who in the Hebrew Bible could be a role model for a man today? There is one person in the Torah who embodies the Yiddish word *mensch*. He is one of the most mysterious figures in the Bible. He is a man of the shadows. He has the ultimate walk-on part in the entire Torah. He is a tender messenger of righteousness and hospitality. His life is a witness to change and a love song to the God of Israel. The implications of his biography jump from the ancient pages into our own time. He is Jethro, the father-in-law of Moses.

When we first meet Jethro, he is a *kohen Midian*, a priest of Midian. Here we learn something interesting. What significance is it that Jethro is a priest of Midian? Consider the words of Genesis 25:2. They come to us, almost as an afterthought, after the death of Sarah, Abraham's wife. "Abraham took another wife, whose name was Keturah. She bore him Zimran, Yokshan, Medan, *Midian*, Ishbak, and Shuach." Midian is a child of Abraham and his new wife. This means that Midian is the stepbrother of Isaac, and that the Midian-ites are a "stepbrother" people to the Israelites. It means that when Moses and Jethro meet, it is more than a mere loving encounter. It is a family reunion, soldering a tie that had been broken genera-tions before.

Moses rescues the daughters of Jethro from some shepherds who were harassing them at a well. They go home and tell their father, and he orders them to bring this stranger home for a meal. Moses stays with Jethro and takes his daughter Zipporah as his wife. Jethro senses that there is an ache deep within Moses' soul— an ache for his own people. Several chapters later, he persuades him to return to Egypt to see how his people are faring.

For many chapters, we do not hear about Jethro. Throughout the long arguments for the release of the Jews, throughout the plagues, we do not see him. Perhaps he has stayed in the wilderness of Sinai. For that is where we meet him again. It is already after the crossing of the Red Sea. It is after the Jews have defeated the hated Amalekites, those desert raiders who sought to kill the weak and enfeebled. Jethro hears of the wonderful things that God had done for Israel, and so he brings his daughter and his grandsons to Moses. We read of the moving reunion of the two men. And then we learn that Jethro rejoiced in God's kindness, and he blessed God, and he affirmed that the God of Israel is greater than all gods.

Here the rabbis ask: What did Jethro hear that brought him back to Moses? The opinions come fast and furiously. He heard of the successful fight against Amalek—the tribe of desert raiders who had genocidal designs upon the weakened Israelites, answers one rabbi. He heard of the parting of the Red Sea (or the Sea of Reeds), says another. Or perhaps, a third rabbi suggested, he came because of the imminent revelation of Torah at Mount Sinai. Jethro taught the Jews how to praise God, for he praised God publicly even before the Jews did. Jethro also taught the gentle wisdom of seeing oneself as only a piece of a task. He saw that Moses was getting overworked in judging the cases that the people brought him. And so he counseled his son-in-law to appoint sub-magistrates to help him with his caseload. Jethro invents the first court system.

The rabbis say, "Jethro came out of the glory of the world and yet he went into the wilderness." Why? He came to join God. Some rabbis imagine that Jethro is no longer a righteous gentile. He actually joins the Jewish people. One midrash says that it was because he had a midlife crisis. He decides to give up being a priest of Midian. His excuse is poignant: He tells his people that he is getting too old for the job. And so the Midianites ostracize him. They refuse to take care of his flocks, which is why his daughters got stuck doing it in the first place, and that is how Moses met his beloved wife.

This is a man who has questions about his spiritual place in the world. This is a man whose own people abandoned him, who reviled him as a traitor or a lunatic. Jethro was a spiritual seeker, a man of restless yearnings. Says the midrash, he had tried every other god in the world. Finally he decided that the God of Israel was the true God.

What is the end of the story of Jethro? We read in the book of Numbers that Moses tried to convince his father-in-law to accompany the people to the land of Israel. Moses hoped that the old man would be their scout and would show them the way through the wilderness. Moses is offering his father-in-law the opportunity to be another Abraham, to join him in creating a new people. Jethro refused to go with them. The Midrash imagines Jethro saying to his son-in-law: "Let me go back to my own land. Let me convert everyone and teach them Torah. Let me bring them beneath the wings of the Divine Presence." Or could it be something else? As all teachers and parent figures must learn, Jethro knows when distance is a blessing. He needed Moses to learn to lead this people himself.

THE POWER OF A RELATIONSHIP

Jethro is friend, teacher, and counselor. Jethro is the archetypal Magician. More than this, he is the mentor. I once asked a group of men: "Did your mentor ever meet your father? And what happened?" A few men whistled softly. One man spoke for the others: "Yes, it happened, and it was a disaster. My father felt jealous of this other man who was taking so much of my emotional time." Some mentors become the fathers we never had.

What kind of fathering did Moses have, anyway? He never "bonds" with Amram, his Israelite biological father, before his mother sends him floating down the Nile, to be found and adopted by Pharaoh's daughter. Does Pharaoh offer him any paternal or grandfatherly love? No—not in the Bible, and not in the various midrashim and legends that surround Moses' life in Jewish lore.

Consider how Exodus 18 describes the moment when Jethro comes back into the life of Moses—right before the revelation at Mount Sinai.

Jethro, priest of Midian, *Moses' father-in-law,* heard all that God had done for Moses and for Israel His people, how the Lord had brought Israel out from Egypt. So Jethro, *Moses' father-in-law,* took Zipporah, Moses' wife, after she had been sent home, and her two sons of whom one was named Gershom, that is to say, "I have been a stranger [Hebrew, *ger*] in a foreign land"; and the other was named Eliezer, meaning "The God of my father was my help, and He delivered me from the sword of Pharaoh." Jethro, *Moses' father-in-law*, brought Moses' sons and wife to him in the wilderness, where he was encamped at the mountain of God. He sent word to Moses, "I, *your father-in-law Jethro*, am coming to you, with your wife and her two sons." Moses went out to meet *his father-in-law*; he bowed low and kissed him; each asked after the other's welfare, and they went into the tent.

Moses then recounted to *his father-in-law* everything that the Lord had done to Pharaoh and to the Egyptians for Israel's sake, all the hardships that had befallen them on the way, and how the Lord had delivered them. And Jethro rejoiced over all the kindness that the Lord had shown Israel when He delivered them from the Egyptians. "Blessed be the Lord," Jethro said, "who delivered you from the Egyptians and from Pharaoh, and who delivered the people from under the hand of the Egyptians. Now I know that the Lord is greater than all gods. . . ."

Next day, Moses sat as magistrate among the people, while the people stood about Moses from morning until evening. But when *Moses' father-in-law* saw how much he had to do for the people, he said, "What is this thing that you are doing to the people? Why do you act alone, while all the people stand about you from morning until evening?" Moses replied to *his father-in-law*, "It is because the people come to me to inquire of God. When they have a dispute, it comes before me, and I decide between one person and another, and I make known the laws and teachings of God."

But *Moses' father-in-law* said to him, "The thing you are doing is not right; you will surely wear yourself out, and these people as well. For the task is too heavy for you; you cannot do it alone. Now listen to me. I will give you counsel, and God be with you! You represent the people before God: you bring the disputes before God, and enjoin upon them the laws and the teachings, and make known to them the way they are to go and the practices they are to follow. . . ." Moses heeded *his father-in-law* and did just as he had said. . . . Then Moses bade *his father-in-law* farewell, and he went his way to his own land.

The italics are this author's. There is no other instance in the Bible in which a relationship is as clear as this one. "Moses' father-in-law." Repeatedly! The text wants to teach us something: that this is the most precious relationship in Moses' life. The Moses-Jethro relationship is probably the most important relationship in the entire Torah. It is second only to the relationship between God and the Jewish people. It is the essence of the bonding between men and the bonding between spirits. We can completely understand the emotional, intellectual, and spiritual depth of Moses' relationship with his father-in-law/mentor, Jethro. Men sometimes find that the relationships they develop with their fathers-in-law are of an entirely different magnitude than the ones they have with their own father. But there is more than that. Jethro is the father that Moses never had. He prepares Moses for a relationship with an even more loving, supernatural Father.

The relationship between Moses and Jethro is so important that it becomes a metaphor. It is not only a metaphor for the relationship that will develop between Moses and God, and between God and the Jewish people. It is also a metaphor for the ideal relationship between the Jews and the world—that of teacher, mentor, and adviser.

It is as good as a relationship can get.

"a hero

or sage"

The Rabbis Re-create
the Jewish Man

1

t was a springtime Friday evening in our home, the eve of the Sabbath. I was about eight or nine years old. As we began dinner, the sounds of fifes and drums wafted through the open window. It was coming from the direction of the schoolyard.

"What is that music?" I asked my father.

"It's the Colonials," he answered.

"Who are the Colonials?" I asked.

"It's a group of kids and adults," he answered. "They dress up in Revolutionary War costumes and they parade around playing fifes and drums. They march in the Memorial Day parade every year," he answered.

This sounded great. I thought of "Warriors of the World," the collection of toy soldiers my parents had reluctantly bought for me. I wanted to join the Colonials.

My mother put her foot down. "Absolutely not!" she said.

"Why not?" I asked her.

She hesitated for a moment, and then said to me: "It's just not what *we* do. We don't glorify war," she explained. There would be no more talk of the Colonials.

My mother never used the term, but she didn't have to. The

unspoken term was *goyim naches*—a Yiddish term meaning a gentile pastime. War, uniforms, fife and drum corps, hunting, dogs as pets, race car driving, Monster Car demolition events—all these things fell into the general category of *goyim naches*. These are things that may or may not be prohibited to Jews according to Jewish law (though hunting certainly is), but things that *culturally* belonged to the gentile world. As a Jewish friend said to me last summer, "I took my son to a demolition derby. I didn't realize that it was going to be an experience in cultural pluralism. We were the only Jews there."

Goyim naches was an exciting category of life, partially because it tended to be physically dangerous. The internalized message was clear: Jewish boys and men do not do this. We do not glorify war. We do not dress up as Revolutionary War soldiers. The French-Jewish photographer Frederick Brenner toured America, looking to see how American Jews had changed. Two photographs stand out: One, a group photograph of Jewish Civil War enactors. Second, a group photograph of Jewish bikers rallying outside a synagogue.

What was the source of my mother's definition of Jewish maleness? It was the history that she—and the Jewish people—had inherited.

The Destruction of Judean Independence: Primal Trauma

After the Romans destroyed Jewish independence in 70 C.E., the Jewish people lost their homeland. They lost their sacred center—the Temple in Jerusalem—their way of connecting to God.

Judaism was a religion that was centered on the *land of Israel* and the *Temple in Jerusalem*. In the wake of the Roman disaster, the Jewish sages did something brilliant. They redefined Judaism and transformed it into a religious system centered in the *home* and in the *synagogue*. The Temple altar no longer existed. The hereditary priesthood of the *kohanim* was now irrelevant. Each man could now be his own "priest" in his own home, the ancient altar magically transformed into the festive table. Jews lacked an altar in Jerusalem upon which to offer the Passover sacrificial lamb. No matter—the telling of the story in the home, centered on an ever-evolving text, became the way to remember the Exodus from Egypt. Once Jews brought sacrifices of grain, incense, and animals to God's dwelling in Jerusalem. Now the offerings were even more precious: prayer, Torah study, and mitzvot, sacred obligations and deeds of kindness.

What became the ideal Jewish male virtues? Virtues that the rest of the world might regard as being *unmanly*—restraint, renunciation, resignation, reconciliation, patience, and forbearance. Why did Judaism encourage such virtues? They were necessary because historical reality demanded them. Judaism became the task of training the heart and the deed—the education toward virtue.

When Jews did not learn about this verbally, they learned it visually. As soon as printers began producing Passover Haggadoth in the later years of the Middle Ages, illustrators looked for ways to portray the Four Sons of the Passover Story: the wise son, the wicked son, the simple son, and the son who doesn't know how to ask. A collection of interesting artistic motifs arose. The wise son was always pictured as a sage; the wicked son was always portrayed as a soldier. That is how the Colonials in the schoolyard became something that was not for me, not for us, not for the Jews.

Transforming Lore: Three Tales

How did the sages accomplish such a remarkable shift in Jewish thinking? As the sole guardians of the Jewish literary legacy, the sages took total control over the management of Jewish lore. They exalted stories of Jewish suffering and martyrdom. The afternoon service of Yom Kippur contains the tales of ten Jewish sages killed by the Romans in the first century C.E. God hears the stories and credits Jews of every generation with the martyrdom of the sages. The stories are not only memory. They are stories of redemption.

The sages transformed necessity into virtue. They deliberately back-burnered—some might even say *censored*—Jewish texts of rebellion and militarism against Rome, stressing passivity and miracles in place of power and self-determination.

HANUKKAH AND THE STORY OF THE MACCABEES

In the third century B.C.E., the entire Middle East fell under the influence of Hellenism. Hellenism was the aggressive exporting of Greek culture—Greek religion, literary forms, art, science, and architecture—into the world. The Greeks were quite successful in this project. In the last few centuries before the Common Era, there was hardly anyone in the civilized world who did not want to become Greek.

There were even many Jews who wanted to be Greek. They were blatant assimilationists, desperately aping Greek ways by changing their names, their language, and their religious norms. The assimilationist position in Judea was strengthened by the decrees of the Syrian king Antiochus, who introduced the worship of Greek gods to Jerusalem. Jewish loyalists, aroused by a priestly family in Modin known as the Maccabees, fought against the Syrians who defiled the Temple, thus winning a decisive battle for Judaism—and by extension, for all of Western culture. For had the Maccabees not won their struggle against the Syrians, Judaism would have perished. In its place would have been the cults of the Greek gods. The Torah would have been forgotten. The names and teachings of the prophets would never even have become known. There would have been no sages of Israel, no rabbinic tradition, no messianic hopes, no Christianity, no Western art, no Western music, no Western culture.

If Judaism had become a casualty of that war, God would have been lost to the world—and the world would have been lost to God.

Consider the way the story is told in the apocryphal book of II Maccabees 10:

When Judah Maccabee and his companions under the Lord's leadership had recovered the Temple and the city [of Jerusalem], they destroyed the altars erected by the gentiles in the marketplace and the sacred enclosures. After purifying the Temple, they made a new altar. Then with fire struck from flint, they offered sacrifice for the first time in two years, burned incense, and lighted lamps. They also set out the showbread [the bread made from grain offerings].

When they had done this, they prostrated themselves and begged the Lord that they might never again fall into such misfortunes, and that if they should sin at any time, He might chastise them with moderation and not hand them over to blasphemous and barbarous gentiles [the standard classical explanation of Jewish suffering at the hands of gentile nations—that it is punishment for Jewish sins].

On the anniversary of the day on which the Temple had been profaned by the gentiles, that is, the twenty-fifth day of the month Kislev [approximately mid- to late December, coinciding with the winter solstice] the purification of the Temple took place.

The Jews celebrated joyfully for eight days as on the Feast of Booths [the harvest festival of Sukkot], remembering how, a little while before, they had spent the Feast of Booths living like wild animals in caves on the mountains. Carrying rods intertwined with leaves, green branches and palms, they sang hymns of grateful praise to Him Who had brought about the purification of His own place. By public edict and decree they prescribed that the whole Jewish nation should celebrate these days every year.

As a child, I learned what most Jewish children learned about the origins of Hanukkah: A jar of oil, sufficient for one day's lighting in the ancient Temple, lasted for eight days. That was the reason for the eight-night celebration of Hanukkah, a celebration which has had its meaning and popularity bolstered by its proximity to Christmas.

But there is no shortage of oil in the version from the book of Maccabees. The oil had no trouble lasting for eight nights. In fact, why did the Jews celebrate the rededication of the Temple for eight days and nights? The text is clear:

The Jews celebrated joyfully for eight days as on the Feast of Booths [the harvest festival of Sukkot], remembering how, a little while before, they had spent the Feast of Booths living like wild animals in caves on the mountains. . . .

The celebration began as a postponed celebration of Sukkot, the eight-day harvest festival celebrated in the early autumn. Why didn't they celebrate Sukkot at its appointed time? Because they were too busy fighting. Why would they bother to celebrate Sukkot beyond its appointed time? It was because the celebration of Sukkot was crucial to an agricultural economy. Without Sukkot, there is no prayer for rain. Without a prayer for rain, there might not be any rain.

Most Jews learn the version of the story of Hanukkah as taught in the Talmud in the tractate *Shabbat*.

Our Rabbis taught: It is incumbent to place the Hanukkah lamp by the door of one's house on the outside [in order to advertise the miracle]; if one dwells in an upper chamber, he places it at the window nearest the street. But in times of danger [persecution] it is sufficient to place it on the table. . . .

What is the reason for Hanukkah? For our rabbis taught: On the twenty-fifth of Kislev commence the days of Hanukkah, which are eight on which a lamentation for the dead and fasting are forbidden. For when the Greeks entered the Temple, they defiled all the oils therein, and when the Hasmonean dynasty prevailed against and defeated them, they made search and found only one cruse of oil which lay with the seal of the High Priest, but which contained sufficient for one day's lighting only; yet a miracle was wrought therein and they lit the lamp for eight days. The following year these days were appointed a festival with the recital of Hallel [psalms of praise] and thanksgiving.

Why the change? Where did the miracle of the cruse of oil come from?

The ancient rabbis opposed the excesses of the Maccabees' descendants, the Hasmoneans, who ultimately assumed power and mismanaged their rule over the Jewish people. They resented the Hasmoneans so much that the dynasty is barely mentioned in the Talmud. In fact, Hanukkah does not even merit its own tractate of the Talmud; the discussion about it is buried, almost as an after-thought, in other tractates. As the haftarah, the prophetic reading in the synagogue, for the Sabbath in Hanukkah, the rabbis chose the passage from the prophet Zechariah, saying that redemptive victory comes "not by might and not by power, but by God's spirit."

Even the hymns of Hanukkah reflect this ambivalence. Con-sider the Hanukkah hymn *Mi Yimalel*, "Who Can Retell?" In the Hebrew version, the song says that *Keyn b'kol dor yakum ha-gibor goel ha-am*—"In every age, a *hero* saves our people." But when the song was translated into English, it was sung, "In every age, a hero *or sage* came to our aid." This is the Jewish moral jour-ney: from the warriors who fought with spears to the sages who fought with Torah—from sword to words. The sages redefined Hanukkah from being a military adventure to being a spiritual adventure—from the miracle of a small army defeating the most powerful empire in the world—to the quasi-miracle of a jar of oil that lasted for eight nights. To this day, Jewish parents protest when I tell the real story.

This was most likely a dangerous distortion. Had the real story of the Maccabees survived, along with the brilliant mili-tary strategies of Judah Maccabee, perhaps the Jews would have maintained their independence. Oddly enough, the Maccabees became heroes—but not to the Jews. They were models for

Christians who were willing to fight and die for their faith. They were often portrayed in medieval Christian art. Judah Maccabee was considered a paragon of knighthood in medieval Europe. His statue stands at West Point—a testimony to his military genius. Decades before Hanukkah would enjoy a newfound popularity in American Judaism, the Maccabee name would resurface in the Maccabiah athletic games for Jewish athletes.

MASADA

In 73 C.E., following the destruction of Jerusalem, a group of Jewish Zealots fled to the deserted fortress of King Herod in the Judean wilderness. That desert fortress is known as Masada. There the defenders committed suicide rather than surrender to the Romans.

The story of Masada is well known today. But here, no thanks can be offered to the ancient rabbis, who were the Zealots' contemporaries. There is no mention of Masada in the Talmud! The story was saved from utter oblivion by Flavius Josephus, the Jewish general-turned-traitor-turned-historian, who recorded the story from the Roman camp at the foot of the mountain. Christians saved Josephus' work, and so the story survived as well.

The story of Masada was dormant within the Jewish imagination until the poet Isaac Lamdan wrote his epic poem about Masada in 1927. Even its site was of relatively recent discovery. Masada did not become a place of pilgrimage until the mid-nineteenth century. Today it is not only a tourist destination, but a place for rites of passage—bar mitzvah, as well as bat mitzvah ceremonies in the fortress's excavated synagogue, and the military ceremonies at which new paratroopers take the solemn vow: "Masada will not fall again!"

But classically, Masada was not part of the foundational myth of rabbinic Judaism. What location took its place? As the late Professor Norman Mirsky noted in his essay "Yavneh vs. Masada," the privileged place of rabbinic Judaism was Yavneh. Every Jewish schoolchild knows the story of how Rabbi Yochanan ben Zakkai was smuggled out of the burning Jerusalem in a coffin. The Roman soldiers wanted to run the coffin through with their spears, but ben Zakkai's colleagues prevailed upon them not to desecrate the sage's body. Once outside the gates of the city, Yochanan ben Zakkai burst out of the coffin and hailed the Roman general as emperor. His greeting of the general as emperor was premature, but only by moments, for a messenger came and told the general that he had been, in fact, elevated to emperor. In gratitude to the rabbi for his sagacity, the new Roman emperor offered him anything he wanted. The rabbi's response is classic: "Give me the city of Yavneh and its sages." Judaism was reborn at Yavneh out of the ashes of the burning Jerusalem. At Yavneh, the Hebrew Bible was finally completed in its final form. At Yavneh, the liturgical forms of Jewish worship took root.

The Torah is often personified as a female—linguistically, it is feminine. The scroll is hidden away in the Ark, like an idealized vulnerable female, and is dressed in beautiful garments; it is removed and paraded around to a waiting congregation, who kiss it. On the festival of Simchat Torah, which celebrates the simultaneous ending and renewal of the Torah cycle, the person who blesses the end of the Torah is called the *hattan Torah*, the bridegroom of the Torah; the one who blesses the beginning is the *hattan Bereshit*, the bridegroom of Genesis. And so, the Yavneh myth created a new kind of Jewish masculinity. If the Torah is personified as a female, and the rabbis successfully rescued Torah, they saved a "damsel in distress"—and with that act, they renewed and continued Judaism.

THE BAR KOCHBA REBELLION

Finally, in 135 C.E., there was an uprising against the Romans by the general Bar Kochba. His strength was legendary. It was said that he could intercept the stones shot by Roman catapults with one of his knees, heave them back, and therefore kill many Roman soldiers. None other than the great Rabbi Akiba hailed him as the Messiah. Bar Kochba was ultimately defeated at Betar. His defeat was to be the last gasp of Jewish independence. But here, too, the rabbinic record is ambivalent (*Lamentations Rabbah* 2:2).

According to Rabbi Yochanan, eighty thousand trumpeters besieged Betar.

Ben Koziva [another name for Bar Kochba] was located in the city, and he had with him two hundred thousand men, each with an amputated finger [As a test of fortitude, he ordered each recruit to cut off a finger]. The sages sent him the message: "How long will you continue to maim the men of Israel?" He said, "How else are they to be tested?" They answered, "Let anyone who cannot uproot a cedar from Lebanon while riding a horse be denied enrollment in your army." Thus, Ben Koziva came to have an army composed of two hundred thousand men with amputated fingers and another two hundred thousand who had uprooted cedars of Lebanon.

Eighty thousand trumpeters entered Betar and went about slaying men, women, and little children, so that their blood flowed in streams out of doorways, even out of grates and pivots. Horses waded in blood up to their nostrils, and the blood flow was so swift that it rolled heavy stones over and over, until the blood finally flowed into the sea and colored the sea. . . .

Now, the Emperor Hadrian owned a large vineyard. They surrounded it with a kind of fence made up of the corpses of Betar's slain, their bodies placed upright with arms spread out. By Hadrian's decree, those corpses remained unburied, until finally another king came to power and ordered their burial.

We are taught: For seven years the nations of the world harvested their vineyards without manuring them, because they were so well fertilized by Jewish blood.

What are we to make of such a horrific account? The sages wanted to emphasize the self-destructive hubris of Bar Kochba. They do not even deign to call him Bar Kochba, the son of a star. To the rabbis, he is Bar Koziva, "the son of a lie." They criticize his mutilation of Jews as a military initiation ceremony. They conclude the story with a gruesome multiplication of Jewish calamity in graphic terms that beggar description.

The Bar Kochba revolt was the last outburst of Jewish rebellion. To this day, Bar Kochba is a code word for military hubris against a superior enemy. The late Israeli military strategist, Yehoshofat Harkabi, penned a crucial book titled *The Bar Kochba Syndrome*, an exploration of how Israeli military policies were pursuing their own version of Barbara Tuchman's "march of folly."

In later years, the early Zionists believed that one of the greatest failures of the Judaism of the rabbis was how they deliberately downplayed Jewish heroism. As the Zionist leader Berl Katznelson would write, "With the loss of political freedom, Jewish historiography lost its freedom as well. . . . The power of forgetfulness and omission in Jewish history is great. . . . That which escaped from external censorship was caught by internal censorship. Did we get any of the Zealots' writings?"

Building a New Jewish Man

A young Jewish college student came to see me. He was having specific problems with his Jewish identity. The conversation started with talk about God, and the truth of Torah, and the need to identify with the Jewish people. But there was more.

"Rabbi," he said to me, pouring out his soul, "I see a lot of the Jewish guys on campus. They whine and they don't stand up for themselves. Why are Jewish guys such . . . well, *wusses?* What does it mean to be a Jewish man these days, anyway?"

This is the definition of manhood that the ancient rabbis bequeathed the world. The first definition of Jewish manhood was *Torah rather than toughness.* In the larger world, macho was the art of brawn. The Jewish critique of macho culture began early. In Roman times, the rabbis forbade Jews from going to the gladiator games, because of their violence. This was the first Jewish critique of the media! And yet there were other rabbis who suggested that it was a mitzvah to go to those games—by doing so, you might be able to give the "thumbs-up" sign and save someone's life. Likewise, in medieval Europe, gentile men engaged in hunting. Jewish law forbade hunting because it was cruel to animals and completely contrary to the teachings of kashrut. Hunting was the realm of King Nimrod, the first mighty king on earth, the prototype of the gentile king, and it was the realm of Esau.

The yeshiva and the synagogue were places of counter-macho. When Jewish men and, increasingly, women put on tefillin, the leather boxes that contain words of Torah, one interpretation says that the straps are to be worn on the weak hand—the hand you use less. Was this but another way to sanctify weakness? Yeshiva students have a strange habit of shaking hands with a limp hand;

perhaps, as the contemporary Jewish thinker Daniel Boyarin surmises, it is their way of creating a counter-handshake in a world
where limp handshakes are looked upon with suspicion, if not
with a certain disgust. Take that same yeshiva student and move
him to the reading desk of the synagogue. There the strong Jew is
the one who can lift the Torah scroll after the reading—especially
when the scroll is turned to either Genesis or Deuteronomy, with
the parchment on either the left or right side, heavily weighing
down the scroll and making lifting a formidable feat. As the Jewish thinker Jacob Neusner has said, Jewish men pursued Torah
study with vigor, strength—and one might even say macho.

This is what I said to the young Jewish college student in my
office. "It's not that Jewish men are wusses. It's that our code of
masculinity is simply different. We demonstrate our masculinity
through a love of ideas and words, an infatuation with argument
and intellectual striving. Some people think that to be a man you
have to know how to go it alone. Not Jewish men. We live like
men in the midst of a community, showing responsibility and living lives of interconnection. Some people think that to be a man is
to 'do what you gotta do.' Not Jewish men. We show that we are
men through a strict adherence to a moral code. It means lifting
ourselves higher than we ever thought possible."

The college student left my office with a new way of looking at
his life and the lives of the other Jewish men he knew. It was a
moment of celebration—a celebration of Jewish difference. Jews
pray differently, study differently, eat differently, live differently.

And if we are men, then we are men differently as well.

israel, our manhood

The Eternal Jew and His Paper Route

It was the summer of 1967—the summer after Israel's stunning victory in the Six-Day War. I remember a Catholic kid at the school lunch table, hearing about the swift Israeli victory, turning to me and saying, "Hey, you guys can really fight!"

On the Golan Heights, maybe. On the Suez Canal, maybe. But back in the middle of Long Island, I was not doing so well against a bunch of Catholic school–educated hoodlums. I had a job delivering newspapers, and the anti-Semitic toughs who hung out at the bottom of my street used to gang up on me.

In order to deliver my newspapers, I had to engage in various forms of subterfuge. I constructed an elaborate network of routes to deliver my papers. I would cut through people's backyards, tunnel through hedges, leave the newspapers at back doors. I would wait until my tormentors would go in for dinner, and then excuse myself from the dinner table and go out to my deliveries. I would then have to weather the complaints of my customers. They somehow thought that an afternoon newspaper should come to their doors, in fact, in the afternoon, and not in the early evening. I lost customers because of it. I was afraid to tell them what was wrong. Once or twice, my customers watched me being beaten up and tormented and found it rather funny. Once, I called the mother of one of the kids on the block, and, doing my best imitation of a woman's voice, tried to pass myself off as the mother of one of the bullies, asking that he be sent home for dinner. Oddly enough, it worked. That is, until the mother on the other end of the phone asked me how my (that is, the other mother's) job interview went. I hemmed and hawed. They actually knew each other! This was a possibility that I had never anticipated! I abruptly said to her, "I don't want to talk about it . . ." and hung up.

So, if one Jewish boy's life is a metaphor for anything, my experience that summer was a metaphor for Jewish history in exile. I was working as a classic middleman, selling goods. In doing so, I was beset by anti-Semites. I was tormented under the watchful and uncaring eyes of neighbors. I constructed elaborate routes of escape. I "suffered" economically due to my victimization. I had to resort to subterfuge and masquerade (over the telephone) in order to "survive." And that my telephone persona was that of a *gentile woman* is simply too funny and ironic even to analyze.

No American Jewish parent wanted a weakling for a son that summer. My father yelled at me: "Go out there and fight those kids!" The hidden translation: If they can do it in Gaza, you can do it on Long Island.

Luck smiled upon me. One day, I discovered that an Israeli teenager was living with a family in my neighborhood as an exchange student. This guy was right out of central casting—well tanned, a *kibbutz* hat, and sandals. As the hour for newspaper delivery would approach, I would sometimes go out on my bike and look for him. Sure, I wanted to hear all about Israel. But I was also hoping that he would hang out with me, walk my route with me, and, if necessary, defend me against my tormentors.

I was the Diaspora Jew who needed the Israeli Jew to defend me. If there had been a contest for poster boy to illustrate contemporary Zionist theory, I would have won.

"Go out there and fight those kids!" my father had yelled. I can still hear him. I could not have known back then that my experience had a particular parallel in the life of Sigmund Freud. In *The Interpretation of Dreams,* Freud writes about how the episodes of childhood often make their way, in well-concealed form, into adult dreams. Freud recalls an incident in his youth when he was ten years old. His father used to take him on walks and tell him that things were much better now than in the old days. The older Freud recalled that when he was a young man, he went for a walk one day with a new fur cap on his head. A Christian came up to him and knocked the cap in the mud and shouted: "Jew! Get off the pavement!" "What did you do?" Freud asked his father. "I went into the roadway and picked up my cap," the older man replied.

The elder Freud's behavior was guided by the way that Jews had lived their lives for centuries in Europe—through the pattern of docility and acquiescence. It is significant, therefore, that in adulthood, Sigmund Freud and Theodor Herzl, the founder of modern Zionism, lived on the same street in Vienna. For Herzl would come to reverse the elder Freud's need to step into the roadway to retrieve his hat.

Zionism as a Masculine Fantasy

Zionism is not *only* the nationalistic enterprise of the Jewish people. It also has a larger significance. Zionism is also a rebellion against the image of the emasculated Jew. It represents a break in the history of Jewish meekness and docility. For Jews, statelessness was the equivalent of frailty; to have a state was not only to come home geographically, but also to come home spiritually and psychically to a new understanding of Jewish strength.

Understand how the fathers of Zionism transformed their movement into a masculine fantasy. Theodor Herzl had been a member of a dueling fraternity at the University of Vienna. Later, he would found his own Jewish fraternity at the university. It had one purpose—to show that Jews could brawl and drink just like any other people.

Herzl fantasized about dueling and defeating Austrian anti-Semites. A duel was not just a duel. Dueling was the symbol of masculine privilege and male honor in Europe. As the late historian George Mosse has written, to duel meant having the same social status as your adversary. As with today's ghetto toughs who will fight if they believe that they have been "dissed," one of the most frequent causes of dueling was the denial of one's due respect. The worst thing was to be called a coward. The dueling scar was a badge of honor. The duel was an accepted part of the lives of military officers, students, politicians, and businessmen—as well as Jews, who used it to disprove the cowardly stereotype of the Jewish man.

That stereotype had gained new power in the aftermath of the infamous Kishinev pogroms, initiated and organized by the local and central authorities, during Easter on April 6–7, 1903. Forty-nine Jews lost their lives and more than five hundred were injured; seven hundred houses were looted and destroyed and six hundred businesses and shops were looted.

In his famous poem, "In the City of Slaughter," the great modern Hebrew poet Hayim Nachman Bialik eulogized the victims of

Kishinev. He described the "lecherous rabble" raping Jewish women. And yet,

> ... *Note also, do not fail to note,*
> *In that dark corner, and behind that cask*
> *Crouched husbands, bridegrooms, brothers, peering from the cracks,*
> *Watching the sacred bodies struggling underneath*
> *The bestial breath,*
> *Stifled in filth, and swallowing their blood!*
> *Watching from the darkness and its mesh*
> *The lecherous rabble portioning for booty*
> *Their kindred and their flesh!*
> *Crushed in their shame, they saw it all;*
> *They did not stir nor move;*
> *They did not pluck their eyes out; they*
> *Beat not their brains against the wall!*
> *Perhaps, perhaps, each watcher had it in his heart to pray:*
> *"A miracle, O Lord—and spare my skin this day!"* ...
> *The* kohanim *sallied forth, to the Rabbi's house they flitted:*
> *"Tell me, O Rabbi, tell, is my own wife permitted?"*

Bialik sneered at pious Jews who could not defend their women. He mocked those Jews who could only hope for a miracle and would emerge from refuge to ask whether their wives were now permitted to them. The wives of *kohanim*, descendants of the ancient priesthood, could not have sexual relations with their husbands if they had been raped. Tragic questions like this would arise after the Holocaust, when Jewish men found that their wives had been drafted into service in the brothels of the SS. Reb Ephraim Oshry, an authoritative decider of post-Holocaust questions of Jewish practice, indeed permitted husbands to resume relations with their defiled wives.

Bialik further lamented how

> ... *The heirs*
> *Of Hasmoneans lay, with trembling knees,*
> *Concealed and cowering—the sons of the Maccabees! ...*
> *It was the flight of mice they fled,*
> *The scurrying of roaches was their flight. ...*

Oy, the poet would ask himself, how is it possible that the descendants of "real men," the Hasmoneans who were descended from the Maccabees, could not fight back? These are Jewish men? Recall that when cartoonist Art Spiegelman drew his famous comic book series *Maus*, the story of his father's experiences in the Holocaust, he chose to depict the Jews as mice. Bialik's poem became a clarion call against Jewish oppression. It sparked political Zionism. Never again would Jewish men—or Jews in general—be passive.

In an odd way, Zionism was a kind of Jewish self-hatred. Jews actually imported anti-Semitic stereotypes from the general culture. In 1898, the Zionist thinker Max Nordau distinguished between the coffee-house Jew and the muscle Jew, and proclaimed that muscular Jews would replace the weak, effeminate Jews of the Diaspora *shtetl*s. The new Jews were to be "deep-chested, sturdy, sharp-eyed Jews." As historian David Biale noted, the early Zionist congresses published postcards with illustrations that contrasted the virile young farmers of Palestine with old, frail Orthodox Jews in the European Diaspora.

Nordau would propose a physical education program for Jewish youth—a program that would build new Jewish bodies to house the new Jewish spirit.

The lionization of the new Jewish man had its ramifications in the early Zionist movement. The early Zionists freely spoke of *muskeljudentum*, muscular Judaism. They believed in revitalizing Jewish manhood. Such a masculine emphasis impeded Jewish women's involvement in Zionism on an equal basis with men. It took an assertive Hadassah movement to trumpet the notion that Jewish women had an equal role in the building of Jewish nationalism.

It also had its effects on early Zionist education. When the early Zionists confronted the totality of the inherited Jewish past, they made choices as to what literary and spiritual areas would be emphasized in the newly settled Land of Israel. In the process, they exalted aggadah, Jewish lore and legend, over halacha, Jewish law. Why? They associated halacha with Eastern European yeshivot, with the ghetto, with weakness, and with pale-faced Talmud students who, let it be recalled from Bialik's poem "In the City of Slaughter," could only ask halachic questions and could not defend their own women. Aggadah, lore, was romantic and inspirational; halacha was the worship of a dead system.

A New Jewish History

Modern Zionism would create a new way of reading Jewish history. The Zionists saw Jewish history as a three-act play. Act One was Jewish history in antiquity. This was a positive time, the period of the Hebrew Bible, an era of national power. Zionism loved biblical heroes such as Samson, Saul, and David, because they were men of power. Zionism loved the Maccabees, and borrowed their name for the Maccabiah Games, the international

Jewish athletic competition that would prove that Jews use their bodies and not just their minds. In Zionist curricula, the Maccabean revolution became the paradigm of a Jewish national liberation movement.

Act Two was *galut*, exile. That act began on the ninth day of the Hebrew month of Av, in the year 70 C.E., when the Temple in Jerusalem was destroyed. *Galut* Judaism was a religion of passivity. The Psalmist had proclaimed that "God neither slumbers nor sleeps." Zionists read that verse and laughed. God had been sleeping all along! And so, instead of applying that text to God, they applied it to Zionist defense organizations. The Hebrew terms of the Bible took on new meaning. When Israel developed its own machine gun, it was named the Uzi, "my power." It is an interesting name for a gun. When the term *uzi* is used in the Hebrew Bible, it always refers to God. God is *uzi*, "my power." No longer. Don't rely on God. Build guns. Prayer won't help you.

Zionists saw exile as bodily pollution or physical disease. Vladimir Jabotinsky was the revisionist Zionist who was the intellectual *zeyde*, grandfather, of Menachem Begin, Benjamin Netanyahu, and Meir Kahane. He founded the militant Betar movement, named for the fallen stronghold of the messianic pretender, Bar Kochba. Jabotinsky often juxtaposed the Yiddish-speaking "Yid" of Europe with the Hebrew-speaking "Hebrew" of the land of Israel: "The Yid is ugly and sickly; the Hebrew has masculine beauty. The Yid is easily frightened; the Hebrew ought to be proud and independent." Jabotinsky admired masculine power so much that his youth organization smelled slightly of fascist youth organizations in Europe. Ironically, German Jewish youth organizations in the 1930s borrowed, ever so slightly and even subconsciously, from German youth organizations of the same period.

Act Three was the homecoming to the land of Israel. To make *aliyah*, the emigration to Israel, was to undergo nothing less than a masculine transformation. The great Israeli poet Uri Zvi Greenberg would write of "masculinity rising in the climate of the land of the prophets/And I was born in Poland a soft child of Judaism and my father's oldest son."

In *galut*, the text for study was Talmud. In Israel, the text for study would be the land itself—its flora and fauna. There, *tiyul ha-aretz*, touring the land, would replace rabbinical literature as a subject of intense intellectual scrutiny. And if there was going to be any kind of traditional text study, it would be the Hebrew Bible. The Hebrew Bible was the text of national power, written for the most part by ancient Israelites who had their own kingdoms. The Jews of the modern land of Israel were no longer "Jews." That term was for Europeans. The Bible never called its characters "Jews." The new Jews would be powerful biblical "Hebrews" once again.

In the words of the old Zionist song *"Anu Banu Artza"*: "We have come to the land, to build *and to be rebuilt* by it."

A Mama-Loshen for Mama's Boys

A people needs a language. The Jews (or, to be precise, Ashkenazic Jews) had two—Yiddish and Hebrew. They were more than simply languages. They were entire models of being in the world.

Yiddish and Hebrew existed in a binary relationship. Yiddish was for profane matter; Hebrew was for the sacred. Yiddish was for the unlearned. Hebrew was for the learned. Hebrew was for men, and in the popular imagination, Yiddish was for women. It was *mama-loshen*, "mama-language," a language that spoke of the comforts of home and mother, that stood in contrast with the more demanding and awesome Hebrew. Jewish women were, in fact, the main readers and consumers of Yiddish. An inscription on the gravestone of the Yiddish writer Sholom Aleichem says that he was "a simple Jew who wrote Yiddish for women." Yiddish books often begin with the explanation they were written for "women *and men who are like women*"—for men who are uneducated! In classic Jewish life, to be effeminate is to be uneducated!

The relationship between Hebrew and Yiddish was a metaphor for the relationship between men and women. Yiddish was a defective language, a stepping-stone in the acquisition of the "real" language, Hebrew—as women were often considered "defective" men. Jewish cartoonists would personify the Yiddish language as an older, plump, maternal woman. A boy at home would only have known the Yiddish of his mother. In order to be a man, you had to leave your mother's apron strings and go out into the world of men and learn Hebrew.

And therefore, Yiddish was the language of Jewish weakness. The late president of Israel, Zalman Shazar, would prematurely eulogize Yiddish by saying: "*Ivrit, lashon kodesh; Yiddish, loshen kedoshim*. Hebrew is the holy tongue; Yiddish is the language of martyrs." When I suggested to our synagogue's Romanian-born, Israeli-bred cantor that we include the classic Holocaust anthem "*Die Partisaner Lied*" ("The Partisan Song") in a worship service, he sniffed, "Yiddish has no place in a Jewish worship service. It is a *galut* language, a language of our exile." And English, I thought to myself, which peppers the Reform service, is *not* a language of our exile? Ah, but English is the language of acculturation, wealth, and power. Yiddish takes us back to the ghetto.

When Israel adopted Hebrew as its official language, it chose the Sephardic pronunciation of Hebrew, as opposed to the Ashkenazic. Scholars believed it was closest to the pronunciation of the Hebrew of national sovereignty in biblical times. But there were more reasons to adopt Sephardic Hebrew: it had been the dialect of the Jews of medieval Spain, who until their expulsion in 1492 had been relatively rich and powerful; indeed, there were even Jewish knights and cavaliers. But the Ashkenazic Hebrew dialect of Central and Eastern Europe sounded weak. It was the dialect of the ghetto Jews, the Eastern European Jews who had gone to their deaths. It sounded a little too much like Yiddish.

And so we have the following dichotomy.

MEN	WOMEN
The Land of Israel	*Galut* (the Diaspora, the exile from the land)
The Hebrew language	The Yiddish language
The *Hebrews* of the Biblical Land of Israel	The Yids/*Jews* of the Diaspora
Study of the Hebrew Bible, Jewish national lore, and a physical love/touring of the Land	Study of Talmud and rabbinical literature
Heroism	Martyrdom

An Exploration of Zionism and Manhood

Years ago, I read a children's book that retold the legend of Captain Jiří and Rabbi Jacob in sixteenth-century Prague. The gentile Captain Jiří did not like that his soldiers were always out carousing. The learned Rabbi Jacob did not like that his students were always being victimized by gentile bullies. Captain Jiří secretly envied the studiousness of Rabbi Jacob's students. Rabbi Jacob secretly envied the fitness of Captain Jiří's soldiers. As the two men slept one night, an angel came and told each man, "Learn from the other." The charming book ends with Rabbi Jacob teaching Captain Jiří's men how to learn, and Captain Jiří teaching Rabbi Jacob's students how to fight.

That's how it was with Israel as well. We would teach the world how to think and read. And the world would teach us how to fight.

Zionism as manhood had many manifestations.

First, there was the way that Israelis dealt with the Holocaust. Israelis were often embarrassed and even hostile toward Holocaust survivors and victims. "Why did they not rebel?" they wondered. The offensive slang term for survivors was *sabon,* or soap—a grisly reference to the soap that was often made of the fat of Jews incinerated in the ovens. As Tom Segev wrote in his penetrating book *The Seventh Million: The Israelis and the Holocaust,* the Zionist goal was to create a new Jewish personality out of elements of "chaos, disfigurement, and both spiritual and physical castration."

Second, there was the way they portrayed themselves in literature. In Aharon Meged's short story, *"Yad Va Shem,* a Memorial and a Name," a young Israeli couple struggles with what to name their newborn son. Their grandfather, a Holocaust survivor, wants the boy to be named Mendel, after the child that he lost in the camps. The new parents are not convinced. Mendel is a name for a weak kid, "a kid with glasses"—a Diaspora Jew. They want to name the boy Ehud, after one of the Israelite tribal leaders in the book of Judges. The biblical Ehud assassinated a Moabite king, Eglon. Mendel is a name redolent of Jewish weakness; Ehud is a name symbolic of Jewish power.

Aharon Appelfeld wrote a short story, "Struck by Light," about a Polish refugee boy who was beaten by other young Israeli Jews because he could not get a suntan. His pallor made them uncomfortable, forcing them to confront the Diaspora and Jewish weakness.

Third, "Zionism as manhood" even appeared in popular culture. Consider the book and movie *Exodus*. Ari Ben Canaan, especially as portrayed by Paul Newman in the movie, is the classic cinematic refutation of the weak, pale-faced yeshiva boy. He is the new Jew—glamorous, blond, Aryan in appearance. In one scene in the film, young Dov Landau is recruited into the Irgun, the underground Jewish militant organization that fought an illegal war against British occupation in Palestine. The Irgun members forced Dov to explain how he survived the horrors of the concentration camp. They poked holes into the various stories that he told them. Finally, he broke down and cried, revealing that he had spent the war as an unwilling sexual partner in an SS brothel: "They used me as you would use a woman!" At that moment, he consented to join the Irgun. It was the only way he could reclaim his damaged masculinity.

Meir Kahane and the Jewish Defense League— A Case Study

Zionism as manhood took on particular importance after the Six-Day War in 1967. The Six-Day War's victorious conclusion transformed the image of the beleaguered Jew into the powerful Jew. Jewish studies programs were growing on campus. The metaphor for those times was the poster of the Hasid in a Superman suit emerging from a phone booth. The Jews were emerging from the phone booths of the world. The Jews were Clark Kents no longer. And yet when you looked closely at that popular poster, you noticed that the Hasid's hands were filthy. Was that an anti-Semitic allusion, or the realization that it is hard to be powerful and keep your hands clean?

It was the dawn of what author Paul Breines calls the "tough Jew." The toughest Jew of them all was Rabbi Meir Kahane, the founder of the Jewish Defense League.

The Jewish Defense League was formed in 1968, the year of the New York City teachers' strike, which first brought militant black anti-Semitism to the foreground. The JDL was a Jewish version of the Black Panthers. Its original goal was to protect elderly Jews from street crime in the racially changing neighborhoods of Brooklyn and Queens. They were the forgotten Jews—those Jews whose children and grandchildren had abandoned them when they migrated north to Westchester and east to Long Island.

The members of the JDL were quite different from most Jews we knew. They were from a different world. They were from Crown Heights rather than Roslyn Heights. They went to Brooklyn College rather than Brandeis University. Their world was the subway. They were the children of the urban lower middle class, the Jewish working class, the outer-borough kids, the Jewish kids who grew up in rowhouses in Canarsie and Pelham Parkway and Rego Park. A fire burned within them. It was nothing less than the fire of Auschwitz that many of them had inherited from their survivor parents.

The only time I saw and heard Meir Kahane was in 1969. He was speaking at my suburban synagogue on Long Island, and was debating another rabbi, a Reform rabbi from a leafy Connecticut suburb. Kahane came with his Jewish Defense League boys. These were not like Jewish kids that I knew.

Kahane spoke about the Holocaust and the lack of Jewish resistance. He spoke about Jewish pride and the need for Jews to defend themselves against their oppressors—whoever and wherever they might be. He sneered at ineffectual Jewish men—"nice Irvings," he called them—lawyers and accountants and men who had done well in college. (He was laughing at our fathers and uncles.) He railed against establishment Jewish groups who cared more about propriety and dignity than about Jewish survival. At the age of sixteen, I had no idea who the Jewish establishment was, much less that I would someday be considered part of it, but then and there I knew that I was against it.

Meir Kahane's message thundered to the ceiling of the social hall: "Never again!" Never again would Jews go meekly to their own destruction. Never again would Jewish boys and girls be nice. Kahane did not believe in niceness. JDL posters ridiculed "nice Jewish boys." Niceness, Kahane said, had led to Auschwitz. I can still hear him saying: "When Moses encountered the taskmaster who was beating a Jew, he did not form a committee. He did not take out newspaper ads. He did not collect signatures on a petition. He slew him."

Who could follow an act like Kahane?

The other rabbi had little to say in response. It was pathetic. Someone asked him about his response to anti-Semitism. He answered that he advocated picketing country clubs from which Jews were restricted. The audience howled with laughter. *Country clubs?* Jews in the outer New York City boroughs are endangered and you dare speak of country clubs?

It was no contest. Meir Kahane won the debate hands down. For two hours, he radicalized that group of suburban Jews. Kahane described the Catskills camp that the Jewish Defense League operated to teach self-defense to young Jews. The Catskills! The summer address of American Jewish vulgarity and excess! A skinny kid from the youth group, himself a scion of a family that owned a famous Catskills resort, pounded his fist into his palm and exclaimed, "That did it. That's it. I'm going!" He was not the only one who went for the sales pitch. For many young Jewish men, tired of being wimps, the JDL was like a Charles Atlas bodybuilding program for the psyche.

The Jewish Defense League began with noble intentions—to protect endangered elderly Jews. When black militants demanded reparations from whites for slavery, and chose to come to New York's wealthy Congregation Emanuel, the JDL was there on the steps to meet them and repel them.

But soon the JDL turned to higher forms of mischief and mayhem in support of Jewish causes. In the words of Yossi Klein Halevi, they had a certain "ecstasy of rage." In the name of Soviet Jewry, they would violently disrupt events featuring Russian performers. In 1972, they placed a bomb in Sol Hurok's office that would kill a Jewish secretary. Judge Jack B. Weinstein's decision in *U.S. v. Kahane, 1971*, in which the JDLers were sentenced on bomb-making charges, was apt: "In this country, at this time, it is not permissible to substitute the bomb for the book as a symbol of Jewish manhood."

Chapter 1 of the JDL was watching out for *bubbes* and *zeydes* on the streets of Flatbush. Chapter 2 was throwing stink bombs at Russian ballet dancers. Chapter 3 happened in Israel. There the JDL moved, along with its leader, and like many new immigrants, changed its name. The JDL became Kach International. Kach, a cold monosyllable, from the Hebrew word meaning "thus it is." There Kahane developed his ideology that blended ultranationalism with fundamentalism. There his followers operated in the West Bank. In ancient cities straight out of Genesis—places like Hebron, where the patriarchs and the matriarchs are buried, the first Jewish acquisition of land in Israel; Shechem, where Joseph's brothers stripped him of his coat and cast him into a pit—Kahane's followers would harass and even physically attack elderly Arabs.

Thus Kahane's moral journey—from protecting elderly Jews in Brooklyn to victimizing elderly Arabs in Hebron and Shechem.

And in This Corner, Goldberg!

There is a flow to the history of Jewish masculinity. In biblical times, Jewish men had power—a tempered power, but power nonetheless. In rabbinic times, the sages recast Jewish heroism. When the Temple was destroyed, the Jewish hero was transformed from warriors to students of Torah. Zionism reversed the switch. Israel became the vicarious masculinity of the Jewish people.

The role model was no longer the Talmudic sage. It was now Moshe Dayan. He was not a Jew with glasses, worn because of congenital eye weakness. He was a Jew with an eye patch who had lost his eye fighting against the forces of Vichy France during World War II. Moreover, his style of scholarship was masculine. It was archaeology—an upper-class, British gentleman's craft, and one that was truly adventurous. Archaeology is an Israeli national obsession because it is Jewish scholarship, not a ghetto scholarship of text, Torah or Talmud, but of the trowel. It is a scholarship of digging in soil, getting your hands dirty—something American Jewish men would never do—and of physical exertion.

Even among the Orthodox, the transformation was real. The pale yeshiva student of Eastern Europe first had to emigrate to Meah Shearim or the Old City in Jerusalem. But one *aliyah* was not enough. He had to move again—this time to the West Bank, where he would learn how to hold an Uzi with one hand and wind tefillin with the other.

Only in a post-Israel world could we encounter someone like the current reigning World Championship Wrestling heavyweight champion. He is a six-foot-four-inch, 285-pound man known as Goldberg. His real name is Bill Goldberg, a thirty-one-year-old son of a Harvard-educated doctor and classical musician. He was once a defensive lineman for the Atlanta Falcons. He wrestled his title away from Hulk Hogan. Crowds cheer him on: "Goldberg! Goldberg!" His signature finishing move is a body slam called the Jackhammer.

As Rabbi Irwin Kula of CLAL, the Center for Learning and Leadership, has said, classically, Jews wrestled with their identity, with text, with meaning, and with God. Goldberg's victory is a Jewish victory. Hulk Hogan is an Aryan symbol. Wrestling is no longer a "goys will be goys" phenomenon. Goldberg says, "Look at us! We're not ototo oververbalized! We're not weak or wimpy! We're the heavyweight champ!"

We know what it means to be Jewish when we're the victim, but what does it mean to be Jewish when you're the heavyweight champion? We're still figuring it out.

iron jew?

Anti-Semitism and the Jewish Man

A few years ago, the Israeli government made a controversial decision to open a tunnel in the Old City of Jerusalem—a tunnel that Palestinians believed to pass directly beneath some of their holy shrines. As one of my female congregants said to me, "That Bibi! He's so macho! What could be more macho than aggressively entering a tunnel?" Not wanting to get into a discussion of the Freudian implications of the Palestinian-Israeli crisis, I simply smiled at that comment and went on ruminating about other matters.

I appeared on national television (MSNBC) with a Christian minister and a Muslim leader to discuss that decision. Everything was going well, until the point in the conversation when the Muslim representative reached across the table and pulled off my eyeglasses, saying, "The Israelis have been stealing from the Palestinians, like I am now stealing your glasses."

I could not believe how angry I was. The man had not only invaded my personal space. He was also was acting out a subtle— or not so subtle—form of anti-Semitism. There I was, a forty-something grown-up Jewish kid with glasses. I was the smart Jewish kid—smart, but not strong. Perhaps in this man's memory there was the image of the patriarch Isaac, blind, lying on his deathbed while his sons quarrel over his blessing—a symbol of Jewish impotence. Freudian analysts would say that when men dream of broken or lost glasses, it is a symbol of the fear of castration. Just great!

Perhaps somewhere in this man's historical memory was an entire genre of medieval Christian iconography (though how it would have gotten there is beyond me). In numerous statues, stained-glass windows and illuminated manuscripts, we find the popular image of *Ecclesia et Synagoga*—"the Church and the Synagogue." The Church, Christianity, was portrayed as a beautiful, erect woman. The Synagogue, Judaism, was portrayed as a blindfolded woman with a broken sword—an impotent, feminized Judaism that was blind to the Christian truth.

Whether he knew it or not, the Muslim leader was doing two things simultaneously: By removing my glasses, in a Freudian sense, he was castrating/feminizing me. He was also emphasizing that I and, by implication, the State of Israel and the entire Jewish people were blind. At that moment, I became the local representative of the blind, effeminate Jewish people.

Am I reading too much into this small, hostile gesture? All I know is that for the first time since I was twelve years old, I asked myself, "Can I take this guy?" I wanted to hit him. However, good Jewish boy that I was, I couldn't. After all, I was on national television. What would they think?

So I did the next best thing. I fought back the Jewish way. With the ghosts of generations of Jewish comedians before my eyes— Jewish men and women who had mastered the art of standing, alone and vulnerable, before a potentially hostile audience—I slugged him with satire. I calmly turned to him and said, "Sir, you are making a *spectacle* of yourself!"

The one-liner had its desired effect. The studio audience convulsed in laughter and the Muslim gentleman thoroughly lost his train of thought. It was a bull's-eye. I retaliated with the classic Jewish weapon—wit and punning. I had won—Jewishly.

The Pathetic Jewish Man?

Historically, anti-Semitic iconography reveals an ambivalent attitude toward Jewish men. Since Jews were considered evil and in league with the Devil, it was easy to portray Jewish men as being ugly. In various visual forms, Jews were portrayed with sallow complexions, hooked noses, hollow eyes, and prominent chins. Jews were said to be unclean and were thought to have spread disease—most notably the Black Plague of the fourteenth century. In later centuries, Jewish men were accused of transmitting venereal diseases; the accusation returned several years ago in Chicago, when black militants accused Jewish doctors of infecting blacks with AIDS.

Jewish men were also considered effeminate. It was not only non-Jews who harbored these images of Jews. In 1869, a noted nineteenth-century Viennese rabbi and scholar, Adolph Jellinek, wrote an ethnological study of the Jews. In his study, he portrayed the Jew as inherently female, and the Jews as the feminine nation among the nations. Jellinek even noted that bass voices are notoriously absent among Jewish men! Like women, Jews are inherently creative, poetic, and docile: "The Woman is happy when she pleases a man and the Jew when he is praised by the non-Jew."

When Jewish speech patterns were burlesqued in late-nineteenth-century cartoons, Jewish men were portrayed as speaking with lisps, leading to a general blurring between Jewish and homosexual stereotypes. It is interesting, therefore, that the revival of Yiddish culture has come from gay and lesbian Jews. A few years ago, a klezmer band, the Klezmatics, released a collection called *Shvaygen = Toyt* ("Silence = Death"), the motto of gay and lesbian activists. The band added a couplet to the solidarity song, *"Alle Brider"* ("All our Brothers"), which referred to *alle freilach*—"all gays." Yiddish is the classic Jewish language of *galut*, exile—and gays and lesbians see themselves as in exile.

The image of the effeminate Jew finds its crescendo in the radical self-hatred of the Austrian Jewish psychologist and philosopher Otto Weininger (1880–1903). On the day that he received his doctorate in 1902, Weininger converted to Christianity. His major work, *Geschlecht und Charakter* (1903, published in English as *Sex and Character*, 1906) was a philosophical justification of male superiority, anti-feminism, and anti-Semitism. After its publication, Weininger succumbed to depression and committed suicide.

Weininger believed that every human being combined male and female elements. Man was the positive, productive, logical, and spiritual force. Woman was the negative force incapable of these virtues. Resorting to a version of the familiar Madonna/ Whore dualism, Weininger believed that Woman is either interested purely in sexual pleasure, the Prostitute, or in procreation, the Mother. As a result, Woman depends on Man and on the Phallus. Her emancipation, as well as the spiritual progress of Man, depends upon sexual intercourse.

For Weininger, the Jew was the Woman, and the Aryan was the Man. The Jew is a force within people that is utterly lacking in belief—like the Woman. Weininger believed that Talmudic discourse was quintessentially feminine, being associative in its form of logic. Weininger believed that Judaism was a belief in nothing, in contrast to the faith in Christianity. For that reason, the Jew gravitates toward communism, anarchism, materialism, and atheism. Zionism, Weininger claimed, could come about only after the rejection of Judaism—the Woman faith.

The Jew as Hyper-Male

But on the other hand, Jewish men were also imagined as *hypermasculine* and *hypersexual*. In late medieval and early modern Europe, Jewish men were considered dangerous to Christian women. Eighteenth-century English caricatures show Jewish men haggling over Christian slave women and seducing Christian girls. Jewish men were often portrayed as perverse, even as child abusers.

In the Middle Ages and in early modern times, Jewish men were liable for strict penalties if they had sexual intercourse with Christian women—penalties that Hitler would later revive. Nazi Germany created its own anti-Semitic pornography, complete with Jewish men raping Aryan women. A cartoon from the Nazi magazine *Der Stürmer* shows a Jew crucifying and raping a Christian woman.

According to Edward J. Bristow in *Prostitution and Prejudice: The Jewish Fight Against White Slavery, 1870–1939,* Jews were involved in the international "white slavery" trade—so much so that Jewish women's groups raised the matter for discussion. In the late 1800s and early 1900s, this concern exploded into anti-Semitic hysteria. Jews were rumored to drug teenage girls and kidnap them. In 1927, a German film on the dangers of white slavery featured a trafficker with stereotypically "Jewish" features. White slavery became the sexual version of the medieval blood libel.

The Nuremberg Laws of 1935 prohibited intermarriage between Jews and Christians, as well as sexual intercourse between Jews and non-Jews, which was branded as *Rassenschande,* "race defilment," and liable to severe punishment. A subtle war was waged against Jewish genitalia. In the horrendous, unspeakable "medical experiments" conducted in the concentration camps, a favorite form of torture was the castration of Jewish men. In his novel *The Far Euphrates,* Aryeh Lev Stollman tells the ultimate story of this horror. The book features a Canadian cantor's sister who wears a cross and pretends to be a Christian—until it is revealed after her death that she had, in fact, once been a man and was castrated in the camps during a medical experiment. Ever since then, she had lived as a woman.

Jewish Male Vulnerability as Metaphor

Thirteen years ago, when my wife, Nina, was pregnant with our first child, we went to a Bob Dylan concert at Madison Square Garden in New York City. The volume of the music was overwhelming. Nina felt our unborn Samuel dancing in the womb, and we were somewhat nervous that the volume of the music could be dangerous to him.

Moreover, there were some guys in leather jackets standing right in front of us. We couldn't see a thing. I asked them several times to move out of our line of sight, but to no avail. Finally, one of them turned around, walked toward my wife, and lifted his third finger at her in the traditional gesture of ultimate disdain. He looked at me out of the sides of his eyes, mocking me. It was as if he were saying, "You want me to get out of the way? Well, I'm giving your wife the finger. What are you gonna do about it?"

We sat back and enjoyed the rest of the concert as best as we could. For the past thirteen years, I have wondered: Was I supposed to get into a fight back then? Did I miss my cue or something?

I was having a "Diaspora Jewish moment." No big surprise— Jews have always been vulnerable in the Diaspora. But the symbol of Jewish vulnerability has often been the vulnerability of the Jewish woman, and the heightened symbol of that vulnerability is the frequent inability of Jewish men to defend their women.

It is as old as the Jewish people. At the very dawn of Jewish history in Genesis 12, Abram and Sarai, whose names will be changed to Abraham and Sarah, heard God's command to migrate to the land of Canaan. But immediately upon arriving in the land of Canaan, they experience a famine, and they leave the Land and initiate the centuries-old rhythm of *aliyah*, emigration to the land of Israel, and departure.

Genesis 12:10–20 states:

There was a famine in the land, and Abram went down to Egypt to sojourn there, for the famine was severe in the land. As he was about to enter Egypt, he said to his wife Sarai, "I know what a beautiful woman you are. If the Egyptians see you, and think, 'She is his wife,' they will kill me and let you live. Please say that you are my sister, that it may go well with me because of you, and that I may remain alive thanks to you."

When Abram entered Egypt, the Egyptians saw how very beautiful the woman was. Pharaoh's courtiers saw her and praised her to Pharaoh, and the woman was taken into Pharaoh's palace. And because of her, it went well with Abram; he acquired sheep, oxen, asses, male and female slaves, she-asses, and camels.

But the Lord afflicted Pharaoh and his household with mighty plagues on account of Sarai, the wife of Abram. Pharaoh sent for Abram and said, "What is this you have done to me! Why did you not tell me that she was your wife? Why did you say, 'She is my sister,' so that I took her as my wife? Now, here is your wife; take her and begone!" And Pharaoh put men in charge of him, and they sent him off with his wife and all that he possessed.

Abram/Abraham is fearful that his wife's beauty will provoke the Egyptians, the paradigmatic powerful foreigners, to take her and to kill him. Abram essentially sells her to Pharaoh. He was afraid that he could not defend himself or her honor.

The biblical story of the rape of Dinah by a Canaanite prince (Genesis 34) is the ultimate parable of Jewish powerlessness in the Diaspora.

The story is worth retelling. In Genesis 34, Dinah, the daughter of Leah and Jacob, goes out and is raped by Shechem, a Canaanite prince. Her brothers are outraged, and they retaliate against Shechem's clan. The brothers' response is telling: "Should our sister be treated like a whore?" Dinah's brothers see the attack on their sister as an attack upon them. Rape, therefore, is connected to the self-esteem of the male.

In his autobiography, *Power Struggle*, the radical Jewish theologian Richard Rubenstein says that there must have been no greater humiliation that a Jewish male could have been forced to endure than to stand helplessly by while his wife, daughter, or sister was raped by gentiles.

For me, it is impossible to think of anti-Semitism and the image of Jewish manhood without thinking of the state of Israel.

Centuries of Jewish passivity came to an end in May 1948, when the state of Israel was born. Never again would Jews have to sketch maps to scoot through the neighborhoods of the world, fearing both the blows of the anti-Semitic bullies and the laughter of the apathetic neighbors.

It was as if a bodybuilding manual had arrived at our doorsteps. For the past fifty years, we have been tearing off the plain brown wrapper. And we have stopped being afraid.

the

struggle

within

Lust and Sexuality

A friend begins the conversation with the following story.

"So we're at a convention, and she starts coming on to me. I'm married and I love my wife, and yet here's this woman, and I'm momentarily infatuated and I'm saying to myself, Why not? Who would it hurt?"

"So, let me ask you the big question. *Why didn't you?*" I reply.

"You really want to know?"

"Sure," I say.

"On the one hand, my wife would kill me if she found out. It would hurt our marriage. Maybe therapy would clean that up eventually. Maybe not. But that's not the point. Bottom line: God didn't want me to do it."

It is not easy. As I write these words, sexuality is very much back in the news. It seems as if it has never *not* been in the news, but now it looks like men's sexuality is under increased scrutiny and judgment. The permissive 1960s and 1970s have given way to a new Victorianism. The Clinton scandal, dubbed by some as sexual McCarthyism; the increased frequency of sexual-harassment suits in private industry and government; changing rules and roles—all these leave men with swimming heads.

Men are drowning in confusion. Once upon a time, and not too long ago, it was acceptable to date a colleague at work. After all, if our generation was going to spend more time at work, then where else would you have the opportunity to meet someone? Now you're looking at sexual-harassment lawsuits, possible dismissal, and public disgrace. Before, if a man made a sexual advance that was not on the menu for the evening, the worst-case scenario was a slap in the face. Now, it sometimes seems as if every amorous touch requires a new set of negotiations. Some militant feminists say that any kind of sexual activity between men and women is a kind of rape. Some men feel, as do even some women, that men are increasingly being painted as Bad Boys. There have even been cases of three-year-old boys hugging girls in nursery schools and being labeled as junior sexual harassers! "Woman, good; man, bad" is the new message. Men keep hearing, "You just don't get it!" Most likely, many men don't.

Where in this contemporary morass can Judaism offer a fresh, redemptive voice?

Sex Is a Good Thing

Let's get it straight. Some ancient philosophical and religious traditions had problems with sexuality. Greek philosophers taught that sex interrupted the time available for intellectual discourse. Early Christianity idealized celibacy. But Judaism has always believed that marital sex is good. Jewish law specifies that husband and wife should make love on a regular basis. Judaism believes that marital sexuality is more than good—it is *kadosh,* or holy.

To paraphrase Rabbi Michael Gold, in the contemporary world, sex is often considered to be a man's right and a woman's duty. Judaism would reverse that. In Judaism, sex is a woman's right and a man's duty. If a man fails to satisfy his wife sexually, she could request a divorce. The question "Was it good for you?" is, therefore, a religious question. Jewish law requires a man to initiate sex with his wife whenever she desires it. Jewish law limits the amount of time that men can abstain from sexual relations with their wives, and such abstinence is permitted only if the husband's trade requires traveling away from home. In fact, a man can take a job that requires increased absence only if his wife permits him to. Jewish law makes it clear—if the wife prefers more of her husband to having more money, the family would simply learn how to make do with less income.

It's not only the sexual act that is at issue here. It's how it was done as well. Sex was supposed to be playful, erotic, imaginative, and spontaneous. There was the free-flowing sensuality and eroticism of the Bible's Song of Songs. The Name of God is not mentioned in the Song of Songs. But the great Rabbi Akiba believed that the holiest day in Jewish history was the day that the Song of Songs was revealed to Israel. Other sages believed that the Song of Songs *was*, in fact, the very Name of God!

A JEWISH SEX MANUAL

You can go to any bookstore and hang out in the sexuality aisle, thumbing through the books, furtively looking at the pictures and diagrams.

Or, you can get your hands on a bona fide Jewish sex manual. It is called *Iggeret Ha-Kodesh*, "The Epistle of Holiness." It is a mystical work, written anonymously in the thirteenth century— some say, wrongly, by the great medieval sage Nachmanides.

The book deals with the challenges of leading a moral family life. Its major area of emphasis is how a pious Jew should have sexual intercourse with his wife. The author teaches this: If you engage in sexual intercourse according to Jewish law and traditions, then your sexual activity in the marriage bed has cosmic implications.

> **The union of a man with his wife, when it is proper, is the mystery of the foundation of the world and civilization. Through the act they become partners with God in the work of creation. This is the mystery of what the sages said: "When a man unites with his wife in holiness, the Shechinah [the feminine Divine Presence of God] is between them in the mystery of man and woman."**

Jewish mystics believed that God had both a masculine persona—the *tiferet*, or "splendor"—and a feminine persona, usually called the Shechinah, the Wandering Indwelling Feminine Presence of God. Because of the exile of the Jews from the land of Israel, *Tiferet* and Shechinah are separated from each other. But through Torah study and doing mitzvot, the masculine and feminine aspects of God can be reunited.

When husband and wife make love on the Sabbath, it is as if a primordial separation between the two of them becomes healed. **"Male and female God created them,"** says Genesis. Each one of us, according to some interpretations, is created male and female. At birth our personae are split, and we spend our lives looking to complete ourselves. And so the masculine and feminine elements within husband and wife become united.

But that union might, indeed, spark a cosmic union as well. When a man and a woman join together in intercourse, it is as if the masculine and feminine mystical attributes of God are joining together in the heavens. The Shechinah, it is said, hovers over the marital bed. Sex, therefore, is more than sex. Sex is how we on earth can bring repair to the Divine Self. We have much more power than we ever knew.

But the Shechinah has a tough sister. That sister is Lilith, the first wife of Adam.

In the book of Genesis, there are two conflicting accounts of the creation of man and woman. In chapter one man and woman are created together, both from the same red earth: . . . "male and female God created them" (Genesis 1:27).

Then in chapter 2 we have the well-known story of Eve being created from Adam's rib. This account seems to contradict the story in chapter 1. The rabbinic solution was to teach that these two chapters are really two different stories describing the creation of two different women—Lilith and Eve.

The rabbinic legends tell us that Adam and Lilith were created as equals from the same red earth. Lilith was beautiful beyond words, with long flowing red hair and wings. When Adam and Lilith were about to make love for the first time, Adam demanded to lie on top of her during intercourse. Lilith objected, saying, "What am I that I should lie beneath you! Were we not made equal? You lie beneath me!" Adam tried to rape Lilith and she, uttering the secret name of God, flew away to the Red Sea, where she gave birth to a thousand demon children every day.

Adam complained to God, "The woman you gave me has deserted me!" God sent three angels to the Red Sea to try to persuade Lilith to return to Adam. Lilith refused, saying, "How can you expect me to return and live like a housewife with that man after what I have seen here at the Red Sea? I shall not return."

Lilith's punishment would be that one hundred of her demon children would die every day. She would seduce men in their dreams, and would have the power to kill little babies up to the day of circumcision for boys and up to the twentieth day for girls. But Lilith had to swear that if she saw a red ribbon and an amulet bearing the names of the three angels in the nursery, she would flee.

God made a new woman out of Adam's rib and called her Eve. God dressed Eve in a bridal gown before bringing her before Adam. Some legends say that God braided Eve's hair for the "wedding"—imagine God as a bridesmaid!

Eve is the "good wife" whom men marry. Lilith is the tougher, more sexual wife that men think they want to marry. Lilith is the consuming, sexually potent woman, and Eve the nurturing mother. They are sides of each other: the one who gives birth (Eve), and the other who murders children and whose fecundity is grotesque (Lilith).

In the same way, the Shechinah is the "good wife." She is loving and longs for us. On the other hand, Lilith has great sexual power. A Talmudic law forbids a man to sleep alone in a house because Lilith will come to him in the night and cause nocturnal emissions (*Shabbat* 151b). So Lilith is the personified sexual fantasy, because you are not going to have sexual fantasies about the Shechinah, are you? Please.

Lilith has to be tamed. I don't know which writer on the television show *Cheers* named Frazier Crane's cold, hostile, non-sexual ex-wife Lilith, but I am betting that it was a Jewish man with a sense of humor.

The Shechinah accompanied Jews into exile and wept with them and over them. She is the powerless woman. That's good. But Lilith behaves toward a man the same way Jews wished they had behaved toward dominant cultures—with defiance and inner strength.

In our darker moments, Lilith comes to our side.

SOME JEWISH MARITAL ADVICE

Back to *Iggeret Ha-Kodesh*, the Jewish guide to marital intimacy.

Generations of Jewish men probably repeated these words to each other. Perhaps this is what Jewish fathers told their sons on the eve of their wedding night.

When engaging in the sex act, you must begin by speaking to your mate in a manner that will draw her heart to you, calm her spirits, and make her happy. Thus your minds will be bound upon one another as one, and your intention will unite with hers. Speak to her so that your words will provoke desire, love, will, and passion, as well as words leading to reverence for God, piety, and modesty . . .

Therefore, a husband should speak to his wife with the appropriate words, some of erotic passion, some words of fear of the Lord. He must speak with her in the middle of the night, and close to the last third of the night. . . . A man should never force himself upon his wife and never overpower her, for the Divine Spirit never rests upon one whose conjugal relations occur in the absence of desire, love, and free will. The Shechinah [God's Divine Presence] does not rest there. One should never argue with his wife, and certainly never strike her on account of sexual matters. The Talmud tells us that just as a lion tears at his prey and eats it shamelessly, so does an ignorant man shamelessly strike and sleep with his wife. Rather act so that you will warm her heart by speaking to her charming and seductive words. . . . A man should not have intercourse with his wife while she is asleep, for then they cannot both agree to the act. . . . When you are ready for sexual union, see that your wife's intentions combine with yours. Do not hurry to arouse her until she is receptive. Be calm, and as you enter the path of love and will, let her insemination come first.

What do we learn from this?

First, you should have sex in the middle of the night. Later in the night is even better. Why? Because "the end of the night" is a metaphor for the coming of the messianic era—that is, the end of the long night of our exile. Having sex with your wife should be messianic. I know, I know, there are some good jokes here. Second, foreplay is holy. Talk about your passion, and then talk about sacred things. This seems like a perfect mood-killer to me, but then again, some people may like it. Third, both partners must be willing. Willing partners invite the Shechinah into their beds. By the same token, men should not be brutal with their partners. Men should never force their wives to have sex. That is for animals. Fourth, take your time. This is not like rushing through the *minchah* afternoon service. Finally, years before Dr. Ruth ever got around to talking about it, the wife should achieve orgasm first. This is what the text refers to as "insemination."

WHY JEWISH HUSBANDS ARE SUCH A PRIZE

Iggeret Ha-Kodesh makes a big deal about husbands not overpowering their wives. Wife beating is wrong—plainly and simply wrong. In folk sociology, Jewish men don't beat their wives. That's why Jewish husbands are such bargains.

Consider this piece from the *Shulchan Aruch*, the classical and authoritative code of Jewish law:

A man who strikes his wife commits a sin, just as if he were to strike anyone else. If he does this often, the court may punish him, excommunicate him, and flog him using every manner of punishment and force. The court may also make him swear that he will no longer do it. If he does not obey the court's decree, there are some authorities who say that we force him to divorce her, if he has been warned once or twice, *because it is not the way of Jews to strike their wives; that is a gentile form of behavior* (Shulchan Aruch, Even Ha Ezer, 154:3).

Another classic text says:

It is an accepted view that we have to treat a man who beats his wife more severely than we treat a man who beats another man, since he is not obligated to honor the other man but is obligated to honor his wife—more, in fact, than himself. And a man who beats his wife should be put under a ban and excommunicated and flogged and punished with various forms of torment; one should even cut off his hand if he is accustomed to wife-beat. And if he wants to divorce her, let him divorce her and give her the *ketubah* payment. . . . You should impose peace between them and if the husband does not fulfill his part in maintaining the peace but rather continues to beat her and denigrate her, let him be excommunicated, and let him be forced by gentile authorities to give her a writ of divorce.

A contemporary Lubovitcher rabbi recently stated:

Observant religious families are not violent. You don't see violence in these homes. They are more spiritual. When a woman told me her husband abused her, I advised her to observe the Jewish rituals. She was not religious enough. A husband becomes less physical and more aware of the emotional aspects of the marriage relationship when a woman observes the *mikveh* ritual. She became more observant, and now they have a happy marriage.

But denial is not only the river in Egypt down which Moses floated as an infant. An Orthodox Jewish woman writes the following:

He hit me before we married—chased me around the room when I refused to marry him. After we married it was much worse. He drank a lot and took drugs. He became even more violent when he was drinking. He was two different people. In public he was the famous doctor, holier than God, loved by all. In private he was a monster. He absolutely controlled everything.

The story gets worse. She became pregnant with a seventh child; he demanded that she have an abortion; she refused; and he threatened to kill himself, her, and the children if she did not not get rid of the child.

The ugly truth is that wife beating is and has been present in Jewish life—some would say, a clear piece of evidence that Jewish men were not exempt from their own kind of sexual assimilation.

Maimonides, in his classic law code *Mishnah Torah*, actually favored beating a wife who requires discipline for failing to perform her household chores. The *beit din,* the Jewish court, should compel her to do her duty even by using the rod (*Hilchot Ishut,* 21:3, 10).

The text that we quoted earlier from the *Shulchan Aruch* continues:

> But if she is the cause of it—for example, if she curses him or denigrates his father and mother—and he scolds her calmly at first but it does not help, then it is obvious that he is permitted to beat her and castigate her. And if it is not known who is the cause, the husband is not considered a reliable source when he says that she is the cause and portrays her as a harlot, for all women are presumed to be law-abiding. Therefore, penalize him severely whether physically or financially for what has happened. Great repentance is necessary, and deal severely with him in the future as you see fit.

Solomon Luria in *Yam Shel Shlomo,* a sixteenth-century commentary on the Talmud, says that a husband is permitted to beat his wife "in any manner when she acts against the laws of the divine Torah. He can beat her until her soul departs, even if she transgresses only a negative commandment."

There are Italian Jewish texts that indicate that wife beating was sometimes an acceptable part of Jewish family life. In the late fifteenth century, Moses ben Shem Tov ibn Habib, a Portuguese Jewish refugee living in Italy, wrote:

> *If your wife is evil and does not obey*
> *Or serve you, and evil plots she does lay*
> *Know that with a strong stick to a rebellious cow*
> *You can straighten her furrows and she will plow.*

IF PRESIDENT CLINTON HAD
JEWISH ADVISERS . . .

Marital sexuality is a mitzvah. Licit desire is more than licit—it is good and holy and wonderful.

But desire comes with a secret clause: *Desire is not always licit*.

What if President Bill Clinton, a Christian, had turned to rabbis and Jewish teachers for counsel? He would have found a body of teachings quite different from those of Christianity. For instance, the doctrine of Original Sin is based on Eve's giving Adam the apple in the Garden of Eden, a metaphor for the sexual act, wherein all of humanity is tainted. Judaism rejects the idea of Original Sin. President Clinton would also have found that Judaism rejects the idea that sin happens because "the Devil made me do it," for this teaching removes too much responsibility from the individual and puts it all on an external demonic force.

He would have learned that the last southern Democratic President, Jimmy Carter, may have been true to Baptist teaching when he confessed that he had often "lusted in his heart," but that is not the way Judaism reads the sexual instinct. The sages knew that the heart lusts: "Thoughts about illicit copulation are more exciting than the act itself, just as the aroma of meat which is more pleasing than the meat itself" (Talmud, *Yoma* 29a). However, outside of some ultra-Orthodox teachings about so-called *machshavot ʒarot* ("alien, libidinous thoughts"), Judaism is not concerned with lustful thoughts. Lustful *acts* are another thing.

What is the source of lustful acts? Clinton would have learned that the human psyche is comprised of two competing urges: the *yetʒer ha-tov* (the good inclination) and the *yetʒer ha-ra* (the evil inclination, identical with what the Greeks would have called the passions, or what Freud would call the libido).

Those two urges battle within the human soul and spirit. In practical terms, Judaism never bothered discussing the *yetzer ha-tov* that much. The *yetzer ha-ra* was the issue—so much so, that at a certain point, texts just talk about the *yetzer*, which is de facto understood to be the evil *yetzer*.

Perhaps "evil" inclination is not the best way to describe it; perhaps "animal desire" is a better way to think about it. Judaism seems to care the most about those actions that we share with the animals—eating and sex. In both cases, Jewish law tries to raise human beings above the animals. In Genesis, God says: "Let us create man in our image and after our likeness." To whom was God speaking? Was it the royal we? Was God speaking to the angels, asking them to help with the act of creation—a scary thought if you happen to be a monotheist?

Columnist and media personality Dennis Prager offers a wonderful interpretation of the text. God was speaking to the animals that God had just created. God was posing a challenge to the animals: "Let's work together to create humanity. I'll put within each person a sacred piece that comes from Me (the *yetzer ha-tov*). I'll also put within each person an animalistic piece that doesn't bother striving for the highest (the *yetzer ha-ra*). We'll see which one wins the battle."

The impulse is evil, but not because sexual desire is evil. It is evil because illicit sexuality could lead to destructiveness, lawlessness, and flagrant dismissal of societal norms. When Woody Allen was revealed to be having an affair with his adopted stepdaughter Sun Yi, he offered this cold assessment of the situation to *Time* magazine: "The heart wants what it wants."

Yes, it does. But that is not how God wishes us to behave.

Dueling Urges

There are two basic ways of understanding illicit sexual desire—the *yetzer ha-ra*.

The first is a dualistic idea. It sees the *yetzer* as something to be fought.

Christianity says, "Wrestle with the Devil." Judaism would say something different. The *yetzer* starts as an external invader. "When the evil inclination sees a man making eyes at girls, frizzing his hair, and walking with a swagger, it says, 'This one is mine'" (*Genesis Rabbah* 22:6). Let that fellow in and there's no telling what will happen. "Rav Avin said: If a man indulges his impulse to evil in his youth, it will in the end, in his old age, be his master."

Some would say: If you can't fight it, at least be careful with it. Here we recall Woody Allen's quip from his early parody of Hasidic tales: A certain rabbi used to confuse the Evil Inclination by giving up without a fight.

> Ilai the Elder said: When a man sees that his impulse to evil is about to gain mastery over him, let him go to a place where he is not known, put on black garments—indeed, wrap himself entirely in black garments—and if that does not restrain him, do what his heart desires but let him not openly profane the Name of Heaven (Talmud, *Hagigah* 16a).

In other words, get out of town and don't embarrass yourself, the Jewish community, or God. Do what you think you have to do, or what your hormones tell you that you have to do. Just don't bother anyone with it.

The real danger of the *yetzer* is that it becomes a kind of secondary god that lives within you. "There shall no be no strange god in you" (Psalm 81:10). "What is the strange god within a man's body? It is the impulse to evil" (Talmud, *Shabbat* 105b).

But God created the *yetzer*, right? True. God may have created the *yetzer*, but the Talmud says that God regrets having done so.

We, on the other hand, must still battle it.

The classic tale of the Jewish man fighting against the *yetzer* is the story of Joseph's encounter with the wife of Potiphar, from Genesis, chapter 39:

When Joseph was taken down to Egypt, a certain Egyptian, Potiphar, a courtier of Pharaoh and his chief steward, bought him from the Ishmaelites who had brought him there. The Lord was with Joseph, and he was a successful man; and he stayed in the house of his Egyptian master. And when his master saw that the Lord was with him and that the Lord lent success to everything he undertook, he took a liking to Joseph. He made him his personal attendant and put him in charge of his household, placing in his hands all that he owned. And from the time that the Egyptian put him in charge of his household and of all that he owned, the Lord blessed his house for Joseph's sake, so that the blessing of the Lord was upon everything that he owned, in the house and outside. He left all that he had in Joseph's hands and, with him there, he paid attention to nothing save the food that he ate. Now Joseph was well built and handsome.

After a time, his master's wife cast her eyes upon Joseph and said, "Lie with me." But he refused. He said to his master's wife, "Look, with me here, my master gives no thought to anything in this house, and all that he owns he has placed in my hands. He wields no more authority in this house than I, and he has withheld nothing from me except yourself, since you are his wife. How then could I do this most wicked thing, and sin before God?" And much as she coaxed Joseph day after day, he did not yield to her request to lie beside her, to be with her.

One such day, he came into the house to do his work. None of the household being there inside, she caught hold of him by his garment and said, "Lie with me!" But he left his garment in her hand and got away and fled outside. When she saw that he had left it in her hand and had fled outside, she called out to her servants and said to them, "Look, he had to bring us a Hebrew to dally with us! This one came to lie with me; but I screamed loud. And when he heard me screaming at the top of my voice, he left his garment with me and got away and fled outside." She kept his garment beside her, until his master came home. Then she told him the same story, saying, "The Hebrew slave whom you brought into our house came to me to dally with me; but when I screamed at the top of my voice, he left his garment with me and fled outside."

When his master heard the story that his wife told him, namely, "Thus and so your slave did to me," he was furious. So Joseph's master had him put in prison, where the king's prisoners were confined.

It is because of this successful battle with his adolescent urges that the ancient rabbis dubbed Joseph *Yosef Ha-Tzaddik*—Joseph the Righteous One. He was immune to the advances of Potiphar's wife.

Here we can learn from Joseph. When temptation strikes, we can try to be like Joseph.

Was not Abraham found faithful when tested, and it was reckoned to him as righteousness? Joseph in the time of his distress kept a commandment, and became lord of Egypt. Pinchas our father, because he was deeply zealous, received the covenant of everlasting priesthood. [In Numbers, Pinchas the high priest sees an Israelite man and a Midianite woman having illicit sex as part of a huge orgy of idolatry and licentiousness. Incensed, he pierces them both with a spear in flagrante delicto. God praises and rewards him for this action] (I Maccabees 2:53).

True, Joseph is punished despite his good deed. But in reality, that punishment leads to his redemption. It is all part of God's master plan. Joseph is rewarded for his righteousness in a difficult situation. He gains power over Egypt (which in itself must have been rather seductive). It is significant that the above text comes from the book of I Maccabees, which recounts the story of the Maccabees' rebellion against Hellenism. Just as the Jewish loyalists were victorious over the external enemy, the passage teaches that Jews can be victorious over the inner enemy as well.

Moreover, if we are like Joseph, then our minds can rule over our passions. An obscure, apocryphal addition to the Maccabees' saga, IV Maccabees, puts it this way:

It is for this reason, certainly, that the temperate Joseph is praised, because by mental effort he overcame sexual desire. For when he was young and in his prime, by his reason he nullified the frenzy of his passions. Not only is reason proved to rule over the frenzied urge of sexual desire, but also over every desire (IV Maccabees 2:1–4).

There was even a prayer that was read in some ancient synagogues (and later adopted for Christian use) that celebrated Joseph as a role model: "You, O Lord, did not neglect Joseph, but gave him to rule over Egypt—a reward of the self-control that You enable."

How did Joseph do it? How could he have known that adultery was wrong? After all, the Ten Commandments had not yet been given on Mount Sinai. And, one might say, "What if I am not religious and don't believe that adultery is against God's will, because who can prove that God even has a will?"

A very early post-biblical tradition, recorded in the book of Jubilees, a collection of alternate readings of Genesis and Exodus, suggests that Joseph knew an unwritten, inner Torah.

Joseph did not surrender himself but remembered the Lord and the words which Jacob, his father, used to read, which were from the words of Abraham, that no man may fornicate with a woman who has a husband and that there is a judgment of death which is decreed for him in heaven before the Lord Most High. And the sin is written on high concerning him in the eternal books always before the Lord. And Joseph remembered these words and he did not want to lie with her.

There is no such thing as simply doing something because it makes good sense. Joseph could have rationalized a sexual dalliance with Potiphar's wife. Somewhere along the line, God must have revealed divine norms—in this case, to Joseph's father, Jacob.

And what if God failed to appear? So says another tradition: Joseph actually did surrender to Potiphar's wife. He was about to go through with it, but at the last moment, the midrash says, "The image of his father Jacob appeared, and his illicit passion departed from him" (*Genesis Rabbah* 87:7).

Remember what God has said to us. And if for some reason you forget what God has said, the image of your father will speak to you.

Learn to Love What You Can't Destroy

But there is a second view of the *yetzer*. It is a view that says that the *yetzer ha-ra* is necessary, holy in its own way, and wrapped up—in a way that is sometimes indistinguishable—with the good. This is the wisdom that men need in our time—to learn to live with the inner forces of the psyche that we cannot, or will not, destroy.

The *yetzer ha-ra* is necessary for a very simple biological reason.

> After people slew the impulse to the evil of idolatry, they said: "Since this is a time of grace, let us beseech God's mercy against the impulse to the evil of lewdness." They asked for God's mercy and the impulse was turned over to them. A prophet warned them: "Consider carefully. If you slay it, the world will be destroyed." They said: "What should we do? If we kill him, the world will end."
>
> So instead of slaying the impulse to lewdness, they imprisoned it for three days. But then, when a day-old egg was sought throughout the Land of Israel for a sick man, it could not be found. So they said: "What shall we do now? If we slay the impulse, the entire world will be destroyed" (Talmud, *Yoma* 69b).

Since the *yetzer* is the libido, and the libido is necessary for sexual activity, and sexual activity is necessary for reproduction, the world cannot exist without it.

It is not accidental that many great presidents have been libidinous leaders—John F. Kennedy, Franklin Roosevelt, Bill Clinton himself. In fact, there seems to be a high correlation between competent leadership and competent libido—some of our best presidents have been adulterers.

Here, too, the Jewish tradition has something to teach. King David was both a great king and a great lover. He was a man who had many wives, and not all of them were gained in pleasant ways. There is no better illustration of this than the story of King David and Bathsheba. Bathsheba was married to Uriah the Hittite. King David saw Bathsheba bathing on a rooftop, and he desired her. He sent her husband into battle so that he would die and he could possess her. The child born of that union died in infancy.

And yet David is still a great biblical figure. He is eternally *David ha-melech*, King David. A lover, a warrior who could not build the Temple because his hands were too stained with blood, a great king and conqueror—but also the purported composer of many of the Psalms in the Hebrew Bible, the most beautiful religious poetry in the world. As I said to someone mourning the loss of a very problematic parent, we read the Psalms of David at a funeral not because he was perfect, but precisely because he was *not* perfect. We are all mixtures of holy and profane. David is the ancestor of the Messiah because when the Messiah comes we will understand how to see ourselves as whole and holy—and we will understand how all our different pieces of the self fit together.

There's something to it. If you can imagine the human psyche to be an office building, then the good inclination and the bad inclination work in adjoining offices. It's not just libido. It's also ambition and drive. The sages said that without the *yetzer ha-ra*, the evil inclination, the unholy impulse, the world could not exist. "Without the evil inclination, no one would father a child, build a house, or make a career," says the Midrash (*Genesis Rabbah* 9:7).

> The sage Abbaye heard a certain man say to a woman, "Let us get up early and be on our way." He said to himself: "I will follow them to keep them from doing what is prohibited." He followed them through meadows. Then, as they were about to separate, he heard them say, "The company is pleasant, but the way is long." Abbaye had to admit: "If I were in their place, I could not have restrained myself." In deep anguish he leaned against the bolt in a doorway [a sign of depression]. An elder came and recited the tradition: "The greater the man, the greater his impulse to evil" (Talmud, *Sukkah* 52a).

As the contemporary Jewish thinker Daniel Boyarin has noted, the same passion that causes Abbaye to study Torah and become a great man, which for the rabbis always means Torah study, is the very same passion that would have prompted him to have sex with the woman in question.

If everything comes from God, then everything has a spark of goodness in it. Even the *yetzer ha-ra*. God may regret having made the *yetzer*, but God's regrets and the world's reality are two very different things.

About twenty years ago, when I was beginning my studies for the rabbinate in Jerusalem, I found myself in a large bookstore, perusing the latest issue of *Playboy* (I was reading the interview, if you must know). A student at one of the local yeshivot that catered to *baalei teshuvah*, newly Orthodox Jews, happened to walk past me. Recognizing me as a Reform rabbinical student, he sneered, "So this is how young Reform rabbis occupy them-selves?"

My precise thoughts at that moment are unprintable. Instead, I remember answering him by saying, "Silly me—I thought that women's beauty came from God!"

He didn't buy it.

Don't misinterpret me. Reading *Playboy* is not a mitzvah. But as I uttered that comment, I was unwittingly paraphrasing a pas-sage in the Talmud.

"It once happened that Rabbi Simeon ben Gamaliel, while standing on a step on the Temple Mount, saw a heathen woman who was particularly beautiful, and he exclaimed: 'How great are Thy works, O Lord'" (Talmud, *Avodah Zarah* 20a).

This is Rabbi Simeon ben Gamaliel—the sage who was the *nasi*, the head of the Sanhedrin in Jerusalem in the first century of the Common Era. He saw a beautiful gentile woman as he was standing on the steps of the Temple Mount, on his ascent to the holiest place in the world. And he still could not keep his eyes off her! But his attraction to her was (ahem) theological, and so he praised her, quoting the Psalm that speaks of the wonders of God's handiwork in the world.

A colleague told me the following story, also concerning the distraction of beauty.

"You know, I always tell bar and bat mitzvah parents that they should remind their guests that they are coming to a synagogue and that they should address appropriately. By this I mostly mean that the women should not wear low-cut dresses, especially if they are coming up to the Torah to say a blessing. I mean, we're not Hasidim here, but even still, there is such a thing as the Jewish value of *tzniyut,* modesty in dress.

"So, of course, last week a woman came up to the podium, and she was ... Well, almost nothing was left to the imagination. I found myself so distracted by the experience that I had trouble concentrating on my prayers. What should I have done?"

I love questions like that. I reminded him of the advice of the Hasidic rebbe, Menachem Mendl of Kotsk. The Kotsker rebbe said that when you are assaulted by licentious thoughts—also called "alien thoughts"—during prayer, you can do one of two things. You can use all your energy in suppressing the thoughts. Or you can do the opposite. You can allow yourself to descend into the thoughts, own those thoughts, and raise them up and see what is holy within them. Chances are, you'll wind up saying something like, "O God, thank You for beauty such as this in Your world."

"You shall love the Lord with all your heart" (Deuteronomy 6:5). In Hebrew, "with all your heart" is rendered *b'chol levavcha.* The Hebrew word for "heart" is *lev.* But here it is written *levavcha*—with two letter *vets* rather than one.

Why this unusual spelling? It is because we must serve God with both sides of our heart—with the good inclination and, yes, with the not-so-good inclination as well. Both have their own ways of worshiping.

THE DEATH OF THE IMPULSE TO SIN

Oh, yes. It will happen—someday. The ancient rabbis speculate that when the Messiah comes, the evil impulse will be slain. At that time, freely libidinous people will be astonished at how small it really is: "*That's* how small it is? And to think I couldn't over-come it!" At that time, the purer ones will be astonished at how large it really is: "Wow, that impulse for gratuitous gratification is even bigger than I thought. How wonderful that I was able to overcome it!" (Talmud, *Sukkah* 52a).

But until then, we live in non-messianic times. We live in a time when good and evil, selflessness and selfishness, the holy and the unholy come together in mixed packages.

The best thing a man can do is to take this wisdom: Know your *yetzer*. And put the good energy that comes from it to work for you.

And remember the words of the sages: "Who is strong? The one who controls his inner urges" (Mishnah, Avot 4:1).

danger

Men at Work

1 sometimes admire Christian saints; they seem to have no trouble conquering their egos. The late Mother Teresa did not spend her life wondering about her book sales, or about how she looked on television. She transcended that; she followed in a long line of Christian holy people who have gone beyond the self. I wish that the rabbinate was that way. It *should* be that way. Alas, it is not always the case.

A number of years ago, I decided to leave a previous congregation. That decision came at the end of a difficult struggle over the meaning of ambition. I wish that I could say that the struggle is over, but it isn't. I went to a congregation that offered a more attractive community, more professional growth, and a better salary. Some of the congregants at that previous congregation were hurt. They felt abandoned. And so they judged my decision. They decided that it was *unspiritual*. "Rabbis should not be concerned about such things," they said to themselves, and sometimes to me. As lovingly and as patiently as I could, I told them that this was not a Jewish understanding of spirituality. Well, yes, there were some stories of rabbis who sequestered themselves in caves to escape the world. There was an entire sect of men who fled from

Jerusalem to the wilderness by the Dead Sea in Qumran—men who may have been responsible for the writing of the famous Dead Sea Scrolls—who wanted to escape the impurities of the material world. Truth be told, such distancing from real life has more in common with Christian or Eastern spirituality than with Jewish spirituality, and is associated more with priests and monks than with rabbis.

Lusting for More

I have taught that the *yetzer ha-ra* is the evil or unholy inclination, which stands in juxtaposition with the *yetzer ha-tov,* the good inclination. Those forces dueling within us determine our behavior and our ethical choices. The ancient rabbis said that the *yetzer ha-ra* was particularly present when men act out inappropriately in a sexual way. Essentially, then, the *yetzer ha-ra* is the failure to respect personal limits and boundaries. If you accept that definition, then understand that the *yetzer ha-ra* does not always appear as the illicit sexual urge. Sometimes it appears as that piece within us that struggles for more and consequentially deifies work.

To quote the medieval Jewish sage, Maimonides,

Do not say that one need only repent of sinful acts such as fornication, robbery, theft. Just as a person needs to repent of these sins involving acts, so persons need to repent of any evil dispositions that they may have—a hot temper, hatred, jealousy, greediness, quarreling, scoffing, eager pursuit of wealth or honors, and greediness in eating. They are graver than sinful acts for when one is addicted to any such disposition, it is difficult to give them up.

The *yetzer ha-ra*, in whatever form it takes, is both powerful and mercurial. I only learned this while spell-checking the chapter in this book on sexuality. Every time Microsoft Word found *yetzer ha-ra*, it converted it into *jester hara*. Great! *"Jester ha-ra!"* The evil jester!" It reminded me of the demonic clown in Stephen King's *It*. And so it is with the *yetzer ha-ra*. The unholy piece of existence often comes to us as a jester, laughing at our pretensions, giggling at our insistent boundary crossings, at our failure to understand and respect the notion that we are not the center of the universe. The *yetzer ha-ra* keeps us from sensing that we are more than we can produce, more than our compensation packages, and much more than our résumés.

A few years ago, I wrote a book titled *Being God's Partner: How to Find the Hidden Link Between Spirituality and Your Work*. It is a book about the role of spirituality, religion, and values in the workplace. When I would give lectures on the topic of work and spirituality, I would ask the audience, "How many of you here are or have been workaholics?"

Without a moment's pause, any number of people would raise their hands, smiling and giggling, often pointing to friends in the room and urging them to raise their hands as well. I would then segue into some other questions. "How many of you here are alcoholics?" "How many of you are drug addicts?" "How many of you are addicted to shopping or sex?" Those questions did not elicit the same laughter or the same jubilant willingness to identify with the addiction. Quite the opposite. When asked those questions, people tended to focus on their shoes. I would then ask the following question: "So why is the only legitimate, socially acceptable, non-stigmatized addiction in America workaholism? And why do corporations look for workaholics to fill their most coveted positions?"

According to Workaholics Anonymous, if you agree with at least three of the following questions, you are either a workaholic or a potential workaholic:

1. Do you get more excited about your work than about family or anything else?
2. Are there times when you can charge through your work and other times when you can't get anything done?
3. Do you take work with you to bed? On weekends? On vacation?
4. Is work the activity you like to do best and talk about most?
5. Do you work more than forty hours a week?
6. Do you turn your hobbies into money-making ventures?
7. Do you take complete responsibility for the outcome of your work efforts?
8. Have your family or friends given up expecting you on time?
9. Do you take extra work because you are concerned that it won't otherwise get done?
10. Do you underestimate how long a project will take and then rush to complete it?
11. Do you believe that it is okay to work long hours if you love what you are doing?
12. Do you get impatient with people who have other priorities besides work?
13. Are you afraid that if you don't work hard you will lose your job or be a failure?
14. Is the future a constant worry for you even when things are going very well?
15. Do you do things energetically and competitively, including play?

16. Do you get irritated when people ask you to stop working so you can do something else?
17. Have your long hours hurt your family or other relationships?
18. Do you think about your work while driving, falling asleep, or when others are talking?
19. Do you work or read during meals?
20. Do you believe that more money will solve the other problems in your life?

Workaholism is not merely a problem. It is dangerous to your health. It brings in its wake such side effects as heart disease, hypertension, gastric problems, depression, exhaustion, vague feelings of emptiness and detachment, and a lack of meaning.

We live in a wonderful modern world. Women have learned to become workaholics with the same gusto and verve with which they learned to become careaholics and addictive nurturers. But for most of history—at least since the Industrial Revolution—workaholism has been a guy thing. Particularly in times of economic challenge workaholism is not just an addiction. To some, it comes close to being a necessity. A cartoon depicts an affluent older man making a speech at a banquet. He is saying, "Last year, thousands of new jobs were created in this country." The thought balloon over the waiter's head says, "Yeah, and I've got three of them."

Who was the first workaholic in history? Perhaps it was Cain. When Cain killed his brother, Abel, his punishment was the curse that the land would refuse to yield its produce for him. That curse must have forced him to work the land even harder. Perhaps it was Moses, who spent so much time caring for the Israelites in the wilderness that he neglected his own personal needs. His father-in-law, Jethro, reminds him of his impending burnout, and counsels him to create a court system in which there are lesser judges (Exodus 18). In the book of Numbers, Moses himself complains to God that he feels depleted, as though he has "given birth to this people."

In the book of Numbers, Miriam and Aaron castigate their brother Moses "on account of the Cushite (i.e., dark-skinned Ethiopian) woman that he took." The traditional way of understanding this text is that Miriam and Aaron were castigating Moses for three possible reasons. One, taking another wife in addition to Zipporah. However, in biblical times this would not have been such a problem. Having multiple wives was standard practice. Two, taking another wife who was dark-skinned. Three, castigating Moses for taking Zipporah as his wife. Since Zipporah was Midianite, and Midian was in the Arabian peninsula, she would have had dark skin. The last two arguments make Miriam and Aaron appear racist. That would certainly be the simplest way of understanding the text, especially when you consider that God punishes Miriam (and not Aaron!) for her gossip against Moses by afflicting her with a skin ailment that turns her skin into white patchy scales!

But the Midrash teaches that Miriam and Aaron's anger against Moses was based on something deeper. They weren't complaining *about* Moses' wife; they were complaining about how Moses was *relating* to his wife—that while he was performing his tasks of leadership he had been ignoring his role as husband and father.

The ancient rabbis saw themselves as the heirs of Moses. Their mission was to transform the ancient revelation on Sinai into living words for their people. And a small piece of Moses' work habits may have been their inheritance as well. Consider the following passage from the Talmud, *Ketubot* 62b:

Rav Rechumi used to frequent the school of Rava in Mahoza, and he would come home on the eve of the Day of Atonement. Once he became unusually involved in his study. His wife, who was expecting him, kept consoling herself, "He'll be here any minute, he'll be here any minute," but he did not come. She was so disheartened that a tear fell from her eye. Rav Rechumi was at that moment seated on the roof of the house of study. The roof collapsed under him, and he was killed.

You call this a marriage? The rabbi comes home to see his wife only on the eve of Yom Kippur. Since you cannot have sexual relations on Yom Kippur, from a conjugal point of view, the visit is somewhat wasted. And yet we can imagine her on an ancient widow's walk, waiting for him breathlessly. But no—this time Rechumi has become entirely engrossed in his study. Some passage of the text is so fascinating that he just cannot tear himself away. In fact, the word that is used for his attachment to his study is the same word that is used for the mutual erotic attachment of the two lovers in the Bible's Song of Songs. So Rechumi has essentially eroticized his study. He has made it his mistress, like many men do nowadays as their work competes with their wives.

A single tear drops from his wife's eye. Only a single tear! Can this marriage be saved? Apparently not. Mrs. Rechumi is about to graduate from "Torah widow" to just plain old widow. As she squeezes out that single tear, her husband, who is sitting on the roof of the house of study, crashes through the roof and dies.

What kind of marriage is this, and what kind of rabbi is this? Why is he sitting on the roof? Why wasn't he in class? Is it possible that he was never formally enrolled, that he just liked to hang out there? The name Rechumi seems to be related to the word *rechem,* which means "womb," but probably is better translated as "compassion." This is compassion? For whom? For his wife? Why does the roof crash in as soon as she weeps? Is it a judgment on the whole system of study that kept men away from their wives? Is it perhaps a reference to the fact that elsewhere the Talmud says that "a man's wife is, in reality, his home?"

Ambition as the Yetzer Ha-Ra

It's hard to find the biblical origins of ambition. But the rabbis think they have found it. It is in the story of the death of Aaron's sons, Nadab and Abihu, in the book of Leviticus, chapter ten. The two sons died on the exact day that the ancient tabernacle was inaugurated.

> Now Aaron's sons Nadab and Abihu each took his fire pan, put fire in it, and laid incense on it; and they offered before the Lord alien fire, which He had not enjoined upon them. And fire came forth from the Lord and consumed them; thus they died at the instance of the Lord. Then Moses said to Aaron, "This is what the Lord meant when He said: Through those near to Me I show Myself holy and gain glory before all the people." And Aaron was silent.

It is a horrific story. But the questions remain: Why did the sons have to die? Ancient Jewish theology could only imagine that they died as a result of some kind of sin. But what was the sin?

The sons of Aaron got creative or presumptuous. Perhaps their narcissism got the better of them. They needed to make their offerings "special." They had to go beyond what God required. So they offered alien fire—offerings that God really didn't need or want. It was the fire to be better, special, the fire of entitlement. It is only one of many eternal lights that burn within the sanctuary of the human soul.

Was it only the sin of presumptuousness and premature liturgical creativity? My own interpretation is that the alien fire was an internal fire that burnt within them. It was the flame of unfettered ambition. Consider this passage from the Talmud, *Sanhedrin* 52a:

Moses and Aaron once walked along, with Nadab and Abihu behind them, and all Israel following in the rear. Then Nadab said to Abihu, "Oh, that these old men might die, so that you and I will be the leaders of our generation!"

The Holy One, blessed be He, said to them: "We shall see who will bury whom."

Rav Papa said: Thus men say: "Many an old camel is laden with the hides of younger ones."

There was a hierarchy of those who were marching through the wilderness. First, there were Moses and Aaron. Then came Aaron's sons, Nadab and Abihu. And only then did the rest of the Jewish people follow. Yet Nadab and Abihu lusted for power and prestige. Professor Jacob Neusner put it this way: "Here is arrogance. Here is naked careerism. Here is youth humiliating age." But Rav Papa knows better. He knows that there have been countless young men who have lusted for the places of their elders, only to have died—spiritually, at least—in the process. The arrogance of the young men became a fire that ultimately consumed them from within.

As Sam Keen has written, "A man must go on a quest to discover the sacred fire in the sanctuary of his own belly to ignite the flame in his heart." We know this well. It's looking at the guy with the fancier title and the corner office, wondering when he is going to screw up or get fired or retire. It's looking around the staff meeting at the ones with whitening hair, the ones who are slowing down, and coveting their lives—or at least the way we think their lives used to be. For some of my rabbinical colleagues, it is looking at the generation of rabbis who came before us. They were the rabbis who first interviewed us for assistant rabbi positions when we were fresh out of seminary and wearing our new suits. And now we are wondering when they are going to retire so that we could sit in their chairs in their offices and on their thrones in the sanctuary.

None of this—neither workaholism nor ambition—comes without a price. One day, the phone call came for me. It was an invitation to apply for a really big position outside the traditional rabbinate. It was on the other side of the country. I played with the idea for a few minutes. Unfortunately, during those few minutes my older son overheard me discussing it with my wife. He screamed at me: "When are you going to be happy simply with what you have?" He was echoing the rhetorical question of Rabbi Tarfon in *Pirkei Avot:* "Who is wealthy? The one who is satisfied with what he has."

I am not hard-wired for contentment. Neither are many men. Neither are many *Jewish* men.

Traditionally, Jewish men weren't such slaves to ambition. Historically, if you were looking for Jewish models of aggressiveness in the outside world of commerce, you would have to look to Jewish women. Jewish women acted like gentile men in the outside world! They were responsible for much of what we would now call masculine roles. They were often the primary breadwinners in the family, while the husband studied. Jewish law even bent to accommodate this. While traditionally a woman was not allowed to be alone with any man but her husband, this was loosened so that women could take business trips alone and enter gentile homes to sell their wares.

One of the most famous Jewish female workaholics in Jewish history was Glueckel of Hameln (1645–1724), a Yiddish memoirist. Glueckel was born in Hamburg into a prominent family. At the age of fourteen, she married Hayyim of Hameln. When her husband moved to Hamburg, she was his business adviser, even while raising their twelve children. As a result, she was able to carry on his business and financial enterprises after his death in 1689. She was a shrewd dealer in precious stones, and her famous memoirs provide an illuminating picture of the international commerce in precious stones and gold as well as of small-scale trading by German Jews in this sphere.

So what happened? As our great-grandfathers used to mourn: "America the *ganif!*" "America the thief!" America stole it all from us. Back in the *shtetl,* learning and piety were valued. Not so in America. In America, the native capitalist and anti-intellectual traditions conspired to *devalue* Jewish learning. Those who did not work were considered parasites. As the Jewish feminist thinker Aviva Cantor has written, America forced men to measure their masculinity by being a breadwinner and by ascending to the middle class. It is more than simply economic need. There is something deeper as well, something involving the ego. We define ourselves through our work. At the cocktail party, the question "So what do you do?" is far from innocent. It is a labeler or, as writer Tom Wolfe would put it, a "social X ray."

It goes even deeper than that; it is related to eternity. As a forty-something Jewish man said to me the other day, "I am getting to that point in life when I want to know that my work will leave something behind for someone. And I don't mean just money." He was talking about the legacy—about the need to be immortal.

Our synagogue is a converted 1930s estate, originally built of wood that was brought to this country from England. At the foot of the staircase that leads up to the religious school, almost in a place that the eye cannot see, there is a large ancient plank of wood. If you look at it very carefully, you can see the inscription: "Rob Chapman Miller, 1772." Rob Chapman Miller was the captain of the ship that brought the wood for the building to these shores. That was the mast of his ship. He signed it as his own version of immortality. Every man is looking for a mast in his own life to sign.

VICTIMS OF THE SEARCH

Consider the American Jewish addiction to the fast track. The first victim is the family. Many observers say that the traditional family is in crisis. It is, but perhaps not in the way that the Christian Right thinks. Are you looking for the threat to this amorphous thing called "family values"? The real crisis of the family is that we moderns have organized our lives around career and status. The real crisis of the family is that it has become secondary to ambition and vanity.

Why? In *The Time Bind*, Arlie Russell Hochschild wrote that both men and women actually favor the workplace over home. Let's face it—the office is more interesting and more fun than the home. The office is an escape from unwashed dishes, unresolved quarrels, testy tots, and unresponsive mates. And so men escape. They escape with the enthusiasm of Rav Rechumi. Men seem to be hard-wired this way. It is the shadow of the primitive "hunter and gatherer" within our genetic memory. Some of work is just pure testosterone. A man told me that when he lost his prominent job after a long, painful, and public battle, "it wasn't losing the job that got me. It was losing the *battle*. It damaged my sense of manhood."

Some of us had parents who expected us to be *nachas*-producing machines. As one of my religious school students said to me recently: "Face it, Rabbi—for our parents we are merely *trophy children*." For Jews of this generation, the deification of work is closely related to the Jewish people's historical situation. The Jews emerged from the Depression. They emerged from a time when the gates of the Ivy League and the prestigious professions were closed to them. So Jewish men live with a silent, often unacknowledged fear: *If I don't keep it up, I could lose it all and wind up back in the* shtetl. *I must work harder, better, more efficiently. I need a better title, a bigger office, a better desk, a faster e-mail system, a better secretary, more colleagues, more underlings, more.* And soon the wanting hijacks your life. It becomes an addiction. But addictions rarely travel alone. They tend to move in pairs—and sometimes in packs. Workaholism is often attached to another addiction—drugs, eating, sex, steroids, money, or pornography.

Do you want to be successful? Sharpen the knife and put your family on the altar. Several years ago, I was a candidate for a pulpit in a large Sun Belt synagogue. The synagogue president casually said to me, "If you become our rabbi, there are certain sacrifices that we will expect."

"Like what?" I asked him.

"Well, like your family, for one," he replied.

"Sorry," I said to him. "Pay attention to the Torah reading on the morning of Rosh Hashanah, and you will see that God stopped Abraham from sacrificing his son. Our faith doesn't require child sacrifice." Generations of Jewish men have had to learn and re-learn that lesson.

And so, a father sings to his sleeping child:

I have a son, a little son,
A boy completely fine.
When I see him it seems to me
That all the world is mine.

But seldom, seldom do I see
My child awake and bright;
I only see him when he sleeps;
I'm only home at night.

It's early when I leave for work;
When I return it's late.
Unknown to me is my own flesh,
Unknown is my child's face.

When I come home so wearily
In the darkness after day,
My pale wife exclaims to me:
"You should have seen our child play."

I stand beside his little bed,
I look and try to hear.
In his dream he moves his lips:
"Why isn't Papa here?"

When I lecture on the meaning of work in life, I ask my audiences: "When was that song written?" They usually assign it to an anonymous Sensitive New Age Dad songwriter of the 1990s. After all, it sounds like another version of Harry Chapin's "Cat's in the Cradle," about a father who never makes time for his son and then discovers that when the boy grows up and has a family, *he* is now the one ignored.

Wrong. I tell them that the lyrics of the song were originally written in Yiddish. The song is named *"Mayn Yingele"* ("My Little One") and that it was written by Morris Rosenfeld in 1887. I imagine that the father in the song worked in a sweatshop on New York's Lower East Side. He was a slave to his work. Generations later, his great-grandchildren may have moved uptown or to the suburbs, out of the sweatshops and into the high-rise offices of Midtown. Yet, the lament is the same.

When we are young, we believe that there will always be another birthday or game or play or concert to attend for our kids. As we grow older, we realize that this is not the case. Monsignor Tom Hartman told me the story of the IBM vice president who was doing a management seminar and suddenly interrupts his prepared remarks with this aside: "I know what you're all thinking. Each of you is looking at me and envying me. Each of you would like to have my job someday. Well, last week was my oldest daughter's wedding. As I walked her down the aisle, I stopped and realized something. I didn't know my daughter. If any of you would like to trade places with me, be my guest."

JACOB AT THE JABBOK

It's not as if men don't understand the perils of ambition. They do. But understanding it is easier than changing.

Consider the story of Jacob, the patriarch. Many years after he cheated his brother Esau out of the birthright and the blessing as the firstborn, Jacob had to learn about life the hard way. He fled to his family's old homeland in Aram Naharaim (present-day Syria), and there his uncle Laban deceived him, giving him Leah as a wife instead of Rachel, for whom he would work an additional seven years. Jacob raised a family. He became rich in flocks and herds. Then there came the moment when Jacob knew that the unfinished business of his life had caught up with him. Jacob is about to reunite with his brother, Esau. He knows that he must make peace with Esau, and he is frightened.

The encounter happened in the middle of the night. It happened at a place called Machanaim, "the camps" (Genesis 32:23–32).

That same night he arose, and taking his two wives, his two maidservants, and his eleven children, he crossed the ford of the Jabbok. After taking them across the stream, he sent across all his possessions. Jacob was left alone. And a man wrestled with him until the break of dawn. When he saw that he had not prevailed against him, he wrenched Jacob's hip at its socket, so that the socket of his hip was strained as he wrestled with him. Then he said, "Let me go, for dawn is breaking." But he answered, "I will not let you go, unless you bless me." Said the other, "What is your name?" He replied, "Jacob." Said he, "Your name shall no longer be Jacob, but Israel, for you have striven with God and men and have prevailed." Jacob asked, "Pray tell me your name." But he said, "You must not ask my name!" And he took leave of him there. So Jacob named the place Peniel ("face of God") meaning, "I have seen a divine being face-to-face, yet my life has been preserved." The sun rose upon him as he passed Penuel, limping on his hip.

Who was the wrestling partner? One interpretation is that the wrestling partner was the evil inclination—the unsanctified piece of Jacob himself. Jacob realizes that he has two sides to himself—the Godlike and the animal-like, the side that knows no boundaries and can only strive for more. Jacob is at Machanaim—"the camps." Jacob *himself* is two camps. Jacob had to learn how to embrace those two sides of himself. This is what it means to grow spiritually.

Before we can struggle with the dark side of who we are, with what Jung called the shadow, we must first make peace with that dark side. We must understand it, we must know it, and sometimes we embrace it. The Sages said that without the *yetzer ha-ra*, the evil inclination, the unholy impulse, the world could not exist. "Without the evil inclination, no one would father a child, build a house, or make a career," says the Midrash. The evil inclination is not only the urge to do really bad stuff. It is also libido and ego and the striving for power. The rabbis were writing long before Freud spoke about sublimation. They knew that truth. Take the dark pieces of who you are and make those pieces do great things. It is what Hasidism calls *ithapcha*—the transformation of the *yetzer ha-ra* into a positive and constructive force.

Another example of this principle is Oskar Schindler, the great righteous gentile who saved so many Jewish lives. As Liam Neeson, the actor who played him, once said in an interview, "Oskar Schindler was no Francis of Assisi." Oskar Schindler was a capitalist, an entrepreneur, a war profiteer, and an opportunist. He was a man of transactions, a hedonist and a bon vivant. He drank heavily, smoked endlessly, and had two mistresses and three illegitimate children. After the war, he could never run a successful business. In later years his Jews brought him to Israel many times.

When he was depressed and looking for purpose, his Jews got him involved in the German Friends of Hebrew University. Before he died, he requested that they bury him in the Catholic cemetery on Mount Zion in Jerusalem. Schindler was a man of great moral weakness. Paradoxically, that is why he was able to do what he did. Had he been saintly, had there been no egotist in him, he could not have accomplished as much. What does Oskar Schindler teach us? Each of us is a mixture of good and bad, saintly and smarmy, decent and depraved. The question is not how we reach perfection. The question is, how do we take the disparate pieces of our lives and lift them up to something higher and holier?

Everything in Us Is Worth Something

A friend of mine asks me if we could have lunch. In the middle of lunch, he starts complaining to me about a certain college president. "When this president first came to the university, the place was in decline. Well, things are really different now. He's really built it up. The problem is that he has, well, you know, a really large sense of himself, he's constantly running around, and his ambition is absolutely naked."

I said to my friend, "Don't you understand? It's only because of those negative things that he could do the positive things. Every positive quality that he has comes with a negative one as part of the deal, free of charge."

So it is with all of us, right back through history. Was Abraham the patriarch who stood up for Sodom and Gomorrah, or the patriarch who willingly led Isaac to Mount Moriah? Both. Was Jacob the heel who cheated his brother, or Yisrael who learned humility at the Jabbok? Both. Was Joseph the egocentric brat who ratted out his brothers, or the savior of the Egyptian economy? Both. Michael Milken, of financial scandal fame, gave major money to a synagogue in Los Angeles for a high school building. Is Michael Milken an inside trader or an aspiring mensch who cares enough about Jewish education to generously finance it? Both.

Successful trial lawyers cannot be effective without massive egos and a lot of chutzpah. The great teacher cannot impart knowledge without obsessive preparation. The philosopher is often disorganized. The artist cannot create without solitude that shuts out the world. Work too hard on parenting, and your professional life takes a hit. Work too hard at the office, and parenting takes a hit. Every holy thing about us has something unholy that goes with it. Jewish mystics teach that when the world was created, light and darkness were intertwined together. Light emerges out of the darkness. Evil emerges out of good. Good emerges out of evil. This is how we were created. That's the way it is. So use the dark side. Is it really all that bad? Can we learn to love those energies? Can the *yetzer* get us to do important, even holy things? Can it help us transform the world?

Can the world even exist without it? Rabbi Judah said: "The world endures because of three things: rivalry, lust, and mercy" (*Avot deRabbi Natan* 4). Put them together, learn how to use them, and learn how to balance them. Take one away, and the world crumbles into primordial dust. For here, too, there is a stream of Jewish thinking that believes in elevating and sanctifying the competitive piece within. The disgruntled, burned-out royal author of the book of Ecclesiastes muses: **"I have also noted that all labor and skillful enterprise come from men's envy of each other—another futility and pursuit of wind!"** (Ecclesiastes 4:4). The ancient rabbis wrote approvingly of *kinat sofrim*, the jealousy that exists between scribes and sages, because such competition makes sages work harder and produce more Torah, and everyone benefits. It is traditional to begin Torah teaching with a joke. Why? According to Jewish mystical sources, Satan is drawn to holy acts, from which he derives nourishment. He can do this, however, only if there is something impure in the performance of the act. Men are in danger of feeling prideful and egotistical in the act of studying Torah, having feelings of ambition and power on account of their teaching and scholarship. By just telling a joke the forces of Satan can be bought off. You pour your ego needs into the joke, rather than the act of study. Once you have satisfied Satan with a good laugh, you can get down to the real work of holy study.

Everything within us is worth something. Knowing that is the deepest work that the soul can do. In the words of the Hasidic master, Levi Yitzchak of Berdichev: Make peace with your *yetzer ha-ra* and put it to use for the good of the world.

BECOMING ONE

Jacob has two names. The mysterious stranger renames him Israel/Yisrael the God Wrestler. But he is also Jacob/Yaakov, the one who overreached and stole the birthright. The name Jacob never disappears. This was not the case with his grandfather Abraham. He was born as Abram, but when God changed his name to Abraham, Abram disappeared. Not with Jacob. I am two camps, says Jacob. That is the final lesson that Jacob must learn. He must confront his own inner duality. And he must become one.

The Zohar knows something important about existence. It calls this world *alma de-peruda*, the world of separation. When the Torah concludes the first day of creation and says *yom echad*, it doesn't mean "the first day." It doesn't mean "Day One." *Yom echad* literally means "the day of unity." On that day, things were unified. But that was it. Ever since that moment when time was in its infancy, there has been constant separation: Dry land from water; birds and fish from beasts; humans from animals; male from female; sibling from sibling: nation from nation; people from God.

Our goal is to find unity, to atone, to be at one, to be *echad*, to be part of an internal process of the soul that mirrors the external process of history. We daily declare that God is One. But perhaps that is only oneness *in potential*. For as the worship service draws to a close, we pray: *Ba-yom ha hu yiyeh Adonai echad u'shmo echad.* "On that (Messianic) Day, God will be One." No more idolatry! True, but not true enough. On that day, all the names of God will be revealed to be refractions of the One, As Yet Undiscovered Real Name of God. Adonai and Elohim and Allah and the Way will all be revealed to be the same. More than this, God's Name will truly be *Echad*. God will be known as the "Unity That Binds and Bonds All Unities." If God is One, and if we truly know that, then our lives become a conscious imitation of God as its disparate pieces meld together. Our lives are searches for the place within us where professional, father, husband, friend, son, brother—and Jew—come together and speak as one.

When Rembrandt painted Jacob wrestling with the angel, he placed Jacob's head on the chest of the angel. Jacob is exhausted but peaceful, his bearded face the face of the New York City Marathon runner who has just finished. The angel is beautiful: loving, caring, comforting, and no longer confrontational. It is impossible to know if Jacob and the angel are wrestling . . . or if they are dancing. I can hear the angel saying: "Jacob, Jacob. Yisrael, Yisrael. It's all right. You can come home now. It's time to come home." So can we. We can come home to ourselves. When

Jacob's sons come to Egypt to buy grain, they describe themselves as being the son of "a certain man" (*ish echad*). That phrase can also be translated as "a whole man." Yes, they are. They are the sons of a man who is *echad,* one, newly whole after the battles of his life. He is truly one.

A DAY OF ONENESS: SHABBAT

The problem becomes this: How do men—especially Jewish men—create balance in their lives? They need *zones of oneness.* They need sacred, holy places. They need places where they do not see each other as colleagues, competitors, clients, or customers. Jewish men once went to the *shvitz,* the communal steam baths. There they shared their stories—and their joys and their woes. There the millionaire could sit next to the pauper, and their sweat would mingle together. Jewish men also went to *shul;* in those days, it was not "the synagogue" and certainly not "the temple." They went to *shul* to *daven,* to pray. Not all of them, of course. As the old joke puts it, Saperstein went to *shul* to talk with God; others went to talk with Saperstein. There was something else. With the exception of the High Holy Days, when the rich often had better seats and Torah honors, the *shul* was a place where status meant nothing.

My dear friend Irving, may his memory be a blessing, suffered the cruelest financial fate that a man could suffer. He had a successful business, which one day he lost. He then lost his house. His family ultimately had to move into a house owned by a dying synagogue. The rent was subsidized with one proviso—he had to be part of the daily minyan, the prayer service. They needed him because he would be the tenth man required for communal worship. He discovered that he liked it. It restored his sense of self, of being needed. And when he died, the men from the minyan were there for his family as well. The synagogue and the Jewish community needs to be a "third place" for men again—that place that is neither home nor work but where souls are free.

This is precisely why so many men like cigars. It is not a phallic obsession, despite what Dr. Freud thought. When I go to a cigar bar or lounge in a cigar store, nothing comes between me and the other men there. I have heard that women are increasingly taking up cigars, but I have encountered only men in my cigar travels. Suddenly my job, salary, career, and status mean nothing. I have chatted with international jet-setters, with truck drivers, with cops, and probably a few guys who secretly harbored objectionable political and social views. It doesn't matter. The whole subject is the cigar—great cigars, cigar prices, where to get good cigars, and reminiscences of treasured cigar moments. That's the whole thing. Everything else evaporates.

As the kindly rabbi tells his son in Aryeh Lev Stollman's *The Far Euphrates:*

> "Our forefathers originally came not from Canaan, not from an earthly Jerusalem, but from the far Euphrates with its source in Eden, from an impossibly remote and primordial home. We cannot forget it, or ever find it again. I believe this fact has afflicted us to the present day."

Some Jewish men will find places that will become their own private Edens. And those moments will help them remember and yearn for the Eden that exists in the sacred realm of time.

The Sabbath is to time as the Garden of Eden is to history—a time/place of purity and of absolute holiness. Just as Adam and Eve left Eden, never to return, there is something within the souls of men that bids them not to return to the Sabbath, that Eden of time. There is a fear of not working. Both the Greek and Roman philosophers thought that the Sabbath was wasteful, foolish, and inefficient. We have inherited their fear. That fear is what unnerves modern Jews about the seven-day shiva (mourning) period. It used to be that Jews sat in mourning for seven days, seriously curtailing their activity. It became traditional for working men to observe shiva for only three days. Slowly, three-day shiva periods became almost universal among nontraditional Jews. The truth is that we are afraid of being "useless" for a few days. We are afraid of losing our responsibilities, even temporarily. We are frightened of blank, unscheduled time. Not surprisingly, those fears reemerge when we think of retirement. Fear of Sabbath, fear of shiva, and fear of retirement are all wrapped up in one psychic package.

There is also good news. The modest Jewish revival in America has created a revival in the Sabbath. Increasing numbers of young, upwardly mobile Jewish professionals are turning to the Sabbath. It is especially necessary when you have a "24-7" job—a job that requires attention twenty-four hours a day, seven days a week. The Jewish sociologist Stephen M. Cohen has noticed that when people go to synagogue, it is not to pray in the conventional sense but to meditate and relieve the tension from work.

The Sabbath judges civilization. It demands restraint, dignity, reticence, and silent rest. Like all of Judaism, it is a question. "How can I stop creating, stop using, stop having, stop acquiring, and simply start being?"

As Rabbi Harold M. Schulweis writes:

> One day out of seven let us erect a barrier to keep out the culture of business, its toughness, its hardness, its obsessiveness, its competition.

One day out of seven let us close our pocketbooks.

One day out of seven let us liberate "In God we trust" from the dollar bill and put it into our lives.

One day in seven let us halt the motor.

One day in seven let us not purchase what we covet.

One day out of seven let us disconnect the TV, fax, and computer; instead, let us take our time, talking and listening to those whom we love.

One day out of seven let us create the balance indispensable for our sanity, our health, and the solidity of our family lives.

The Hebrew word for Sabbath, *Shabbat*, is a feminine noun. The Sabbath has numerous links to the feminine in Judaism and to the feminine part of human nature. It is personified as a queen or a bride. So, too, it is a day in which men can allow the feminine part of themselves to come out—the piece that is receptive, open, and emotional. It is easy to try to live in perpetual Sabbath. It is tempting to live in a way in which competition has vanished from our lives. Some men succeed. Some men, confronting professional crisis, see that crisis as opportunity. Having been "downsized," they choose to re-create the way they work. Some men go for smaller, lower-paying, less demanding jobs, and find that way of life is a blessing. Some men choose to move from the top of their game to a place or job in which life is easier. They "downshift" or "plateau." And some men reinvent themselves totally, and thus find a true inner peace. They give up the struggle or resolve it.

A colleague tells me about a man in his congregation who was the CEO for a major oil company. He is in his late forties, with one child still in high school and another in college. And yet he grew tired of simply racking up 200,000 miles a year in frequent-flyer points. He became convinced that there was something more to life. He resigned from his job, just wanting to learn to relax, and found a more fulfilling way to work.

The Jewish Sabbath is a foretaste of the Messianic era. The Talmud says (*Berachot* 17a):

> **The future world is not like this world. In the future world there is no eating or drinking or propagation or business or jealousy or hatred or competition, but the righteous sit with their crowns on their heads, feasting on the brightness of the divine presence.**

RETIREMENT AS OBITUARY?

Not long ago, I had lunch with a rabbi in his mid-sixties. He is one of the most respected rabbis in America, with a life full of accomplishments and accolades. "So, when do you think you'll retire?" I asked him. I know how much he loves his summer house, his writing, and various other activities. And yet at the mere mention of the word *retirement,* his face paled and his hands began to shake. "Please, can we not get *morbid?*" he pleaded. "Morbid," which means "deathlike."

Not too long after that, a successful corporate mogul, approaching retirement, was talking about putting up a new building. It would be his last big project, he said. He put it in an interesting way, though: "This will be my last *erection.*"

One speaks of death. One speaks of sexual impotence. It is not accidental that men who have become unemployed become depressed and lose their libidos. These men know the score. They know the external measure of life. Every morning they open the newspaper and notice how obituaries are written. There are two classes of obituaries: Class I is "above the fold," a place reserved for prominent people who have died. In those obituaries, the profession comes first, and the survivors are listed at the very end of the article. Class II is below the fold—the long columns of people's names. There the survivors are listed *first*, and then, after that—*maybe*—we find the profession. So how can Jewish wisdom help us enter retirement?

Rav Soloveitchik: Adam I and Adam II

Many people who read the book of Genesis cannot help but notice that there are two accounts of the creation of humanity. Genesis 1:27–28 states that

> **God created man in His image, in the image of God He created him; male and female He created them. God blessed them and God said to them, "Be fertile and increase, fill the earth and master it; and rule the fish of the sea, the birds of the sky, and all the living things that creep on earth."**

Here we find an Adam made in the divine image, created along with woman and given the task of procreating and dominating the earth.

Then comes the second account of the creation of humanity. According to Genesis 2:7, God **"formed man from the dust of the earth. He blew into his nostrils the breath of life, and man became a living being."** Soon Eve was created from one of Adam's ribs. Some Bible scholars suggest that this is proof of multiple authorship of Genesis. Perhaps they are right. But for the great contemporary Orthodox theologian, the late Rav Joseph Soloveitchik, these two creation stories hint *not* at multiple authors of the

Torah, but at two facets of humanity. Soloveitchik calls these two facets "Adam I" and "Adam II."

Genesis describes Adam I as fashioned in the image of God. Soloveitchik says Adam I is creative, functionally oriented, enamored of technology, and one who seeks dignity by mastering and transforming nature. He is a pragmatic problem solver. He is an entrepreneur, aggressive, and bold. He lives in community with others because community helps bring difficult projects to fruition. He builds, plants, harvests, regulates rivers, heals the sick, and governs. By appraising his handiwork, he imitates God, who evaluated His handiwork at the end of each stage of creation. For Soloveitchik, Adam I is "majestic man." Adam I is the man of competence. His question is: "*How?* How can I achieve these ends, this program, this objective?" These questions are not so bad. But we must be careful. When Adam I is in control, religion and spirituality suffer, because competence and manipulation triumph.

We moderns know this all too well. Our century has witnessed Adam I's greatest triumph as he sought unlimited power. He has imitated the builders of the Tower of Babel, whose apex would pierce heaven. We live in the era of the heaven-piercers, the descendants of Adam I who can only ask the questions: "How? How much? How many?" Adam I's quest has led to widespread environmental despoliation and military technology that can devastate entire cities with the push of a single button. It has brought us the demonic power of Auschwitz. The world has not been the same since we surrendered our civilization to Adam I.

The Adam I of competence needs his counterpart, the Adam II of the spirit. Adam II's major question is not *"How?"* but *"Why?"* "*Why* was the world created? *Why* am I here? *Why* did God give me a special task to perform? *Why* is there suffering?" Adam II submits to God; his relationship with God gives him ultimate meaning in life. True to the description of his creation, he knows that he is dust and will return to dust. Standing in humility and dread before God, he is the religious human being par excellence.

Each of us encompasses both Adams. Sometimes we ask "How?" and sometimes we ask "Why?" Within each of us, Adam I can evolve into Adam II. When the drive for achievement, success, and accomplishment begins to wane around the onset of middle age, Adam II takes over and the search for faith, meaning, and religious community begins to take the ascendancy.

Soloveitchik noticed that this duality presents two kinds of spirituality. There is the spirituality of Adam I, which is based on being competent and in control. There is also the spirituality of Adam II, who, in his trembling before God, is more reflective. Midlife and retirement bring a transition from Adam I to Adam II, from the one who is in control to the one who is capable of mature reflection.

Someone once said that religion is for people past the age of forty-five who are looking back at their lives and wondering about the meaning of it all. Retirement, therefore, is a time for a matured reflection on the meaning of life and the meaning of career and mission.

Isaac's Wells

Consider this seemingly minor incident in the life of Isaac (Genesis 26: 18–22):

> So Isaac departed from there and encamped in the wadi of Gerar, where he settled. Isaac dug anew the wells which had been dug in the days of his father Abraham and which the Philistines had stopped up after Abraham's death; and he

gave them the same names that his father had given them. But when Isaac's servants, digging in the wadi, found there a well of spring water, the herdsmen of Gerar quarreled with Isaac's herdsmen, saying, The water is ours. He named that well Esek [contention] because they contended with him. And when they dug another well, they disputed over that one also, so he named it Sitnah [harassment]. He moved from there and dug yet another well, and they did not quarrel over it; so he called it Rehovot, saying, Now at last the Lord has granted us ample space [Heb. *hirhiv,* connected with Rehovot, to increase in the land].

When I was younger, I read this passage and sighed. Poor Isaac, I thought. The hapless patriarch has almost nothing of his own creation to leave behind. He simply redigs the wells of his father, Abraham, like many of us are afraid of simply reliving our fathers' lives. Now that I am older, I have come to believe that the names of Isaac's wells symbolize something deeper.

Rabbi Yehudah Leib Alter of Ger, the author of the Hasidic commentary *Sefat Emet,* thought that the names of the wells symbolized the progress of the days of the week. *Esek* is the well of striving. *Sitnah* is the well of dissension and hatred. Those are the "wells" of the workday week. But as we approach the Sabbath we move to *Rehovot*—the well of spiritual expansiveness and openness. Now I understand that there is something even deeper in the words of the *Sefat Emet.* The wells do not only symbolize the passage of the week, but the seasons of life. When we are young, we are at the well of *Esek,* "striving." We are working hard. Then we confront the fact that we will not get everything we want out of work and out of life. We begin to realize that there are others who will get the brass ring that we had coveted. And so we journey to the well of *Sitnah*, "dissension" and "hatred." Sometimes we feel that dissension and hatred toward those who have made it, or whom we suspect are our competitors. Sometimes, we turn those feelings of dissension and hatred inward, and those feelings can become corrosive. Then there is a season to move toward retirement. As that journey begins, we discover certain other things within ourselves. We discover new interests and passions. We become more comfortable with who we are. That leads us to the well of *Rehovot*, or "openness"—openness to ourselves and to others.

We want to know that our work means something. We struggle, like Jacob, with the questions "Did my accomplishments add up to anything?" "Was my career worth all the prices that I had to pay?" "Will I be missed?" We want to leave behind a legacy. We want to be a Moses, placing our hands on a Joshua who will succeed us, and bring something of us into a Promised Land that we might not even see. We want to be like the prophet Elijah saying good-bye to his disciple, Elisha, and leaving his cloak and a double portion of his spirit behind as he is swept up into heaven. We want to be like the Hasidic sage who refused to die until he had given the gift of his eyes to one disciple, his mouth to another, his hands to another, and his ears to yet another. We want our lives to mean something.

Before Jacob encountered the nameless stranger at the Jabbok, he forded his family and possessions across the river. "I have sent all that I have across the river," he muses. As we age, we see the river differently. We start to ask: "What do my possessions mean to me?" After we've gotten the Lexus, the promotion, the corner office, and the weekend ski house, there is the question, "Now what?" The truth is that God does not judge us by our salary, job description, or by the size of our offices. We enter our final years knowing the questions that we will hear after we die.

When a person ascends to the ultimate judgment, they ask these questions: "Did you conduct your business with faithfulness to the Jewish ethical tradition? Did you set aside fixed time for study? Did you engage in the mitzvah of procreation? Did you hope for salvation?" (Talmud, *Shabbat* 31a).

People who retire well keep growing. They know that there are numerous seasons in life and that each season yields its own fruits.

All the years of Rabban Yochanan ben Zakkai were one hundred and twenty: forty years he engaged in business; forty years he studied; and forty years he taught (Talmud, *Rosh Ha Shanah* 31b).

The men I know who have entered their twilight years with joy have found another kind of work, volunteer work, charities, and various organizations with which to busy themselves. These tasks bring them to the final well—*Rehovot*, expansiveness. Those men have not shrunken with age. Rather, they have expanded with wisdom.

Reb Nachum, son of the Hasidic Rabbi Israel of Rizhyn, once taught: These are the lessons of checkers. You can't make two moves at once; you can only move forward, not backward; and once you reach the last row, you can move anywhere you want.

the

unkindest

cut?

The Bris Reconsidered

My oldest son, Samuel, will soon become bar mitzvah. My memories go back to those first days when Nina and I first became parents.

It was at Samuel's bris ceremony, on the eighth day of his life. As my wife, Nina, and I prepared to bring Samuel into the ceremony, Nina looked at our eight-day-old baby boy, dressed in the same circumcision gown that I wore and that my father had worn, and said, "We love you, Samuel." There was a sadness in her voice that I had not understood. I have searched for the source of that sadness—and of the sadness that I felt as well.

Everyone senses that brit milah (ritual circumcision, usually known by its Yiddish pronunciation *bris*) has a remarkable emotional hold over Jews. It always has. Baruch Spinoza, the seventeenth-century Jewish philosopher and heretic of Amsterdam believed that brit milah single-handedly guaranteed the continued existence of the Jewish people. But tell that to the "anti-circ" crowd.

The New York Times reported that the rate of circumcision of newborns has dropped to between 60 and 70 percent nationwide. Some worry about the risks of circumcision. Yes, there are risks, but complications are rare—estimated at one in five hundred, and that usually involves local infection and bleeding. A parent would need to weigh such risks against the hygienic benefits of circumcision. Circumcision virtually eliminates the possibility of penile cancer and various bacterial dangers, as well as preventing cervical cancer in women. Yet, to be fair, proper hygiene can achieve the same purposes.

There is more to it than that. "Circumcision is barbaric" groups have become particularly aggressive. According to Dr. Edgar Schoen, a senior consultant in pediatrics at Kaiser Permanente Medical Center in Oakland, California, there is actually a growing trend among affluent boomers that sees the possession of a foreskin as being, well, chic.

So what are the objections to circumcision? Primarily, opponents complain that the baby has no say in the matter. Hanny Lightfoot-Klein, the author of *Prisoners of Ritual*, actually compares male circumcision to clitoridectomy in Africa, a grisly procedure that causes infections and makes sex and childbirth painful. She says, "A cut is a cut. And it's the first cut that cuts the trust between a child and its mother."

Some critics suggest that circumcision inprints violence on the baby's brain, or that circumcision encodes the developing brain with pain. Some go so far as to suggest that this is one of the beginning stages of establishing the sadomasochistic personality. In her book *Banished Knowledge: Facing Childhood Injuries*, psychologist Alice Miller suggests that circumcised men are inherent child abusers because they insist on circumcising the boys of the next generation.

Others say that circumcision diminishes sexual response. Apparently, the foreskin provides the penis with its own self-lubricating, movable skin. "The female is thus stimulated by moving pressure rather than by friction only, as when the male's foreskin is missing," says Dr. Paul Fleiss, an anti-circumcision activist. Some clinicians estimate that there are several hundred nerve endings in the foreskin, each one providing sensual pleasure.

Still other anti-circumcision activists suggest that men are traumatized by the loss of their foreskins, and actually mourn the loss. One man said, "When I first saw the scar on my penis, I felt someone had taken something."

All those complaints about circumcision are reasonable. But they also strike me as being just a little anti-Semitic. Decode them with me.

First, the suggestion that the child has no say in the matter sounds like the traditional critique of Judaism—a wrathful God who must be served, or else. Just as God imposed the Divine will on the Jewish people, parents have imposed their will on their helpless infant. If the child is compelled in infancy to go through life without a foreskin, this is an affront to his religious dignity. But maybe not everything requires the consent of our children.

Second, that circumcision creates a tendency toward violence in children. Well, as we have already seen, Jewish men are typically nonviolent. If circumcision creates a tendency for violence in young males, Jewish history would have been quite different— an epic of marauding, hostile men. How about that it hurts sexual activity? How would we know? Can we imagine Jewish men asking uncircumcised gentiles about their sex lives, and wondering if theirs is measuring up? There is something a little pagan in that argument—that anything that might possibly interfere with maximum sexual enjoyment is evil.

I don't look at the medical data—and frankly, I couldn't care less. The American Academy of Pediatrics has stated that while there are medical benefits of circumcision, there is no justification for it as a routine medical procedure.

This may be true, but it misses the point. For Jews, circumcision is not just a medical procedure. In fact, that's the least of it. The person who performs the circumcision should be a *mohel*, a ritual circumciser who sees this not as surgery, but as sanctity. Actually, in the ongoing debate between going to a pediatrician/urologist versus *mohel*, the *mohel* wins—and even most physicians will agree. They simply perform the procedure more often than most doctors. The British royal family's employing a *mohel* for years to circumcise their sons is enough of a recommendation for most people.

Some things are deeper than the medical aspects of circumcision—for example, culture and memory. When I worked as a rabbi in rural Pennsylvania, every week I would get a call from "hill Jews," as I called them. These were Jews who fled to the shores of the Delaware River to get away from other Jews. "Hello, Rabbi," the call would invariably begin. "You don't know me, but my wife just had a baby boy, and would you happen to know the name of a *mohel?*" There are many Russian Jews who were denied the ability to circumcise their sons until they got to Israel. It was the same for the Ethiopian Jews, who zealously guarded the commandment of circumcision. A Jew would have to be crazy—or, at the very least, very estranged from Judaism and the Jewish people—not to circumcise his or her son.

It's not only with infants. Ritual circumcision evokes something deep in male converts to Judaism, who are traditionally required to go through that process. If they are already circumcised, as most are nowadays, there is the traditional taking of a drop of blood from the penis. It has the same power. I will never forget the day when I witnessed *hatafat dam brit,* the ritual drop of blood, from a male Jew-by-choice. As he, and I, and the *mohel*, and my colleague shared the moment, I admit there was squeamishness, but it was a tribal squeamishness. "Congratulations," we said, in an ancient moment of male bonding, "you are now one of us."

Consider these words from a male convert to Judaism:

It happened on Election Day. It's more a soreness than pain, but it feels like a choice I actually made. I never realized, before tonight, that my conversion was the discovery of my Jewish soul, which started way back in tenth or eleventh grade. A pretty straight line led from "no Jesus between me and God" to learning about Judaism as a culture which still existed in our time, as opposed to the Judaism I learned in Sunday school—that Judaism was the forerunner to Christianity and that Jews had missed the boat about twenty centuries ago. Christianity didn't care what I did, because it was all forgiven in advance, as long as I made the correct affirmations or acceptances. But the Jews' God cared about what I did, not what I thought.

I feel in my flesh that I have made a choice, but maybe I just finally got around to making my flesh conform to my soul, which had already been chosen.

This morning I felt freed. Freed to carry the yoke of heaven.

The ancient rabbis were right when they noted the remarkable sociology of Jewish practice:

Rabbi Simeon ben Eleazar said: Every precept, such as abstention from idolatry and observance of circumcision, for which Israel were willing to die during the Roman Emperor Hadrian's persecution, is still held on to firmly. Any observance for which Israel were willing to give up their lives has been preserved among them. Thus the Sabbath, circumcision, and study of Torah, for which Israel were willing to give up their lives, have been retained by them.

In other words, when Jews died in order to do certain mitzvot, those mitzvot endured in Jewish history—and Jews died for the ritual of circumcision. Anti-Semitic rulers knew its primal power, which is why circumcision was the first Jewish practice they outlawed. Years ago I met a young Jewish boy in Moscow who had been circumcised at the age of three because there had been no way for him to be circumcised during his infancy. Tell that family that circumcision doesn't matter. It does. It is the way that Jewish men have always "looked Jewish"—even and especially in hostile surroundings. Rent the film *Europa Europa*, and watch the odyssey of a young Jewish man in Nazi Europe who tries to hide his circumcision.

The History of Circumcision

How can we explain this tremendous psychic hold of circumcision upon the imagination of modern Jews? What does it truly evoke for them? What is the source of its stubborn popularity, even for Jews who are estranged from everything else in Jewish life?

Circumcision has a long and powerful history. Brit milah is not only the oldest Jewish ritual, it is also the oldest religious ritual in Western religion.

It goes back to God's covenant with Abraham, at the dawn of Jewish history (Genesis 17:1–14, 22–27):

When Abram was ninety-nine years old, the Lord appeared to Abram and said to him, "I am El Shaddai. Walk in My ways and be blameless [or, "be whole"]. I will establish My covenant between Me and you, and I will make you exceedingly numerous."

Abram threw himself on his face; and God spoke to him further, "As for Me, this is My covenant with you: You shall be the father of a multitude of nations. And you shall no longer be called Abram, but your name shall be Abraham ["father of a multitude"] for I make you the father of a multitude of nations. I will make you exceedingly fertile, and make nations of you; and kings shall come forth from you. I will maintain My covenant between Me and you, and your offspring to come, as an everlasting covenant throughout the ages, to be God to you and to your offspring to come. I assign the land you sojourn in to you and your offspring to come, all the land of Canaan, as an everlasting holding. I will be their God."

God further said to Abraham, "As for you, you and your offspring to come throughout the ages shall keep My covenant. Such shall be the covenant between Me and you and your offspring to follow which you shall keep: every male among you shall be circumcised. You shall circumcise the flesh of your foreskin, and that shall be the sign of the covenant between Me and you. And throughout the generations, every male among you shall be circumcised at the age of eight days. As for the homeborn slave and the one bought from an outsider who is not of your offspring, they must be circumcised, homeborn and purchased alike. Thus shall My covenant be marked in your flesh as an everlasting pact. And if any male who is uncircumcised fails to circumcise the flesh of his foreskin, that person shall be cut off from his kin; he has broken My covenant. . . ."

And when He was done speaking with him, God was gone from Abraham.

Then Abraham took his son Ishmael, and all his homeborn slaves and all those he had bought, every male in Abraham's household, and he circumcised the flesh of their foreskins on that very day, as God had spoken to him. Abraham was ninety-nine years old when he circumcised the flesh of his foreskin, and his son Ishmael was thirteen years old when he was circumcised in the flesh of his foreskin. Thus Abraham and his son Ishmael were circumcised on that very day; and all his household, his homeborn slaves and those that had been bought from outsiders, were circumcised with him.

Before Abram/Abraham could fulfill the blessing of fertility and become a "father of nations," his organ of generation must be circumcised—symbolically opened up to procreate the Jewish future. We read that when God was done speaking with Abram, the Holy One was gone. Is brit milah, then, Abram's way of responding to God's perceived absence? Is it Abram's bringing God back into his presence and into history as well? The Israelites who left Egypt and wandered in the wilderness were not circumcised. In order for them to truly "come home" to the land of Israel, as part of the ceremony of covenantal renewal in the book of Joshua, they circumcised themselves. To be uncircumcised is to be the Other. Throughout the Bible, the term "uncircumcised" was a code word for "foreigner." When the book of Exodus describes Moses as a man of "uncircumcised lips," it means that, being Egyptian-reared and Egyptian-speaking, he could neither communicate with his fellow Jews nor have any personal authority over them.

Circumcision was at the root of ancient anti-Judaism as well. The Greeks, who invaded and occupied the land of Judea in the fourth century BCE, did not understand circumcision. To the Greek mind, circumcision violated the perfection of the body. That argument is still with us. One anti-circumcision activist maintains that "circumcision wounds and harms the baby and the person the baby will become. Parents who respect their son's wholeness are bequeathing to him his birthright—his body, perfect and beautiful in its entirety."

In Hellenistic times, the Syrian emperor, Antiochus Epiphanes, outlawed circumcision (I Maccabees 1:48). This was among the many outrages that inspired the Maccabean revolution. Many Jewish mothers who circumcised their sons suffered martyrdom. II Maccabees 6:10 says that two women who had circumcised their children were led around the city with their babes bound to their breasts and then cast off the wall. The omnipresent potential of martyrdom for circumcision testifies to its raw emotional power in Jewish history.

Assimilated Jewish males in Hellenistic Judea wanted to participate fully in Greek culture. This meant participating in the athletic contests in the *gymnasium,* the quintessential Hellenistic institution. Athletes competed naked, to better accentuate the excellence of the male body. Some Jewish men who didn't want to appear different went through the painful process of reversing their circumcisions—having their flesh pulled forward, the true origin of cosmetic surgery!

The anti-circumcision argument in the Greco-Roman period helped the early Christian Church. When Christianity started in Palestine, the only way to become a Christian was to become a Jew first. But when Paul took Jesus' message outside Palestine to the lands of the Hellenistic Diaspora, he encountered a problem. To become a Jew, you had to become circumcised. He discovered that it was impossible to preach about circumcision to a bunch of pagans who believed that their bodies, down to each feature, were inherently sacred.

Paul told potential converts that there was no longer any need for circumcision. Why not? Because the blood of Jesus, shed on the cross, is better than all the circumcision blood in the world! Borrowing a metaphor from the prophet Jeremiah, Paul insisted that the most important thing was circumcision of the heart—the purity of the inner life. In Romans 2, he states: "He is a Jew who is one inwardly, and real circumcision is a matter of the heart, spiritual and not literal."

During the Middle Ages, Jews were frequently accused of killing Christian children and using their blood for wine. The blood libel was also connected to circumcision. In the blood libel of Tyrnava, Slovakia, in 1494, it was alleged that the Jews needed blood because "the blood of a Christian was a good remedy for the alleviation of the wound of circumcision . . . and that the blood of a Christian is a specific medicine for it, when drunk."

As Jews entered the modern age, they discovered new objections to circumcision. Abraham Geiger, one of the intellectual founders of Reform Judaism, thought that circumcision was "a barbaric, gory rite which fills the infant's father with fear and subjects the new mother to harmful emotional strain." The early-twentieth-century sexologist Paolo Mantegazza called upon Jews to "cease mutilating yourselves; cease imprinting upon your flesh an odious brand to distinguish you from other men; until you do this, you cannot pretend to be our equal." Then, of course, came Sigmund Freud. Freud theorized that when little gentile boys heard about circumcision, such reports would create castration anxiety: "Oh, my God, the Jews are going to take a piece of my penis!" That anxiety would lead to more anxiety: "Oh, my God, what if the Jews don't stop with just a small piece of my penis? What if they take the whole thing? Then I will become a woman! And who wants to be a woman? Women are inferior to men! Curse the Jews for making me into a woman!" As Freud saw it, circumcision leads to castration anxiety, which leads to anti-Semitism, which is related to sexism.

Back to Samuel's bris. At the last moment, Nina had said, "We love you, Samuel." She later remembered feeling "like I was carrying my son to a sacrifice."

Perhaps in order to understand circumcision, we must journey to the very depths of what it means to be human. What is the reason for this non-rational, almost mystical attachment to bris? It may reach back into our genetic memories and bring us back to that dark early period of human history when parents sacrificed their firstborn children to the gods. As René Girard wrote in *Violence and the Sacred* (1986), sacrifice sanctifies the human impulse to violence by confining it to a specific time and place and assigning it to a specific set of actors. Ritual circumcision limits it even more. Is circumcision, then, a sublimation of the ancient human desire to sacrifice our children? It may be. That's why my wife and I were so sad. We got it. We felt that we were about to carry our eight-day-old boy to a sacrifice. The ancient, primitive, pre-literate, dawn-of-humanity tribal memory was there.

Circumcision as Sacrifice

This concept—circumcision as sacrifice—is a crucial, compli-
cated, controversial, and murky story. It goes back to Moses as he
receives his commission from God. He is commanded to bring the
Israelites out of Egypt. He and his family are about to return to
Egypt to carry out the mission. Exodus 4:21–26 reads:

> And the Lord said to Moses, "When you return to Egypt, see
> that you perform before Pharaoh all the marvels that I have
> put within your power. I, however, will stiffen his heart so that
> he will not let the people go. Then you shall say to Pharaoh,
> 'Thus says the Lord: Israel is My firstborn son. I have said to
> you, Let My son go, that he may worship Me, yet you refuse
> to let him go. Now I will slay your firstborn son.'"
>
> At a night encampment on the way, the Lord encountered
> him and sought to kill him. So Zipporah took a flint and cut
> off her son's foreskin, and touched his legs with it, saying,
> "You are truly a bridegroom of blood [hatan damim, perhaps
> better understood as "blood relative"] to me!" And when He
> let him [Moses' son] alone, she added, "A bridegroom of
> blood because of the circumcision."

Why is God trying to kill Moses' son? It's as if God were saying, "Moses, Zipporah—you must bring this child into the covenant of the Jewish people. Don't think I've forgotten about that
ancient promise that I exacted from Abraham." God has just told
Moses that even the firstborn of Pharaoh will not be safe. And
now, for some demonstration of God's power, the Holy One goes
after Moses' firstborn—just to show the family what is possible.

Or it may have been to show the family what a little blood can ultimately do. For there is more to the story. At what time of day does this encounter with the Lord happen? It happened in the middle of the night. In the Bible, there are other sacred nocturnal adventures. In the middle of the night, Jacob wrestles with the nameless assailant at the banks of the Jabbok River, and is wounded in the loins. More important, the Exodus from Egypt happens in the middle of the night. The firstborn of Egypt die during the final plague, right before the departure from Egypt. How does the Angel of Death know to avoid the houses of the Israelites during that plague? Because the Israelites have smeared the blood of the Pesach sacrificial lamb on their doorposts.

Perhaps, then, the circumcision passage foreshadows that quintessential moment of national redemption, when the Angel of Death flies over the houses of the Israelites. The blood of circumcision redeems the child from death. It is smeared on his "legs," but "legs" is a biblical euphemism for male genitalia. In both cases, the blood has redemptive power. It is possible that the blood is a sacrificial offering to God. The bris ceremony contains the hopeful words: "Save the beloved of our flesh from destruction, for the sake of His covenant placed in our flesh." The blood saves us—more than we can ever imagine.

The Inner Mystery of Circumcision

However, there is no explanation of ritual circumcision in the Bible. It is a mystery—in the deepest religious sense. What does this mystery say to the hearts and souls of men? Circumcision is humanly performed and therefore unnatural, thus permitting the covenantal partners to transcend nature. Circumcision sanctifies nature by saying that there is a divine force and a command that is above nature. Circumcision allows Jews to become partners with God. A midrash states (*Genesis Rabbah* 11:6):

> A pagan philosopher asked Rabbi Oshaia: "If circumcision is so beloved of God, why was the mark of circumcision not given to Adam at his creation?" Rabbi Oshaia replied: "Observe that every thing that was created during the six days of creation needs finishing: mustard needs sweetening, wheat needs grinding, and even man needs finishing."

In this way we become God's partners in the work of creation. Ritual circumcision happens on the eighth day of the child's life so that the child can live through Shabbat—the octave of the week—and thus is part of the process of creation.

Circumcision is marked in the hidden place of the body. The Torah is also kept in a closed, hidden place in the sanctuary—the Holy Ark. Therefore, our best wisdom about the way to live remains hidden and must be revealed by additional human effort.

Circumcision contains lessons about parental effort and striving. The child bears the mark, but the mark was made by the parents. In just this way, who we are inscribes itself on our children. Circumcision reminds us that our children are a gift, for which we are not ourselves creatively responsible.

The Jews are a tribe. The parents must remember, now when it counts, that they belong to a long line of descent, beginning with Abraham. As novelist Philip Roth wrote in *The Counterlife:* "Circumcision makes it clear as can be that you are here and not there, that you are out and not in—also that you're mine and not theirs. . . . There is no way around it: you enter history through my history and me. Circumcision confirms that there is an us."

Circumcision sanctifies the generations by sanctifying the organ of generativity. The Hasidic master, Rabbi Yehudah Leib Alter of Ger, wrote in his Torah commentary *Sefat Emet:* "The mitzvah of circumcision was assigned to this particular limb, for it is the source of flow and generation." Ritual circumcision is an act of transmission, of *remembering*. When my first son, Samuel, was circumcised, I looked at his penis and said: "From this penis my grandchildren will come."

Circumcision teaches the real meaning of wholeness and holiness. It is one of those glorious paradoxes that are part of the real religious life. In order to be whole, you have to be just a little bit broken. It's why Jacob, the limping patriarch, is the paradigm of the true Jewish hero. It is also why the most famous Jewish baseball players, Sandy Koufax and Hank Greenberg, are more famous for the games that they did *not* play, because they conflicted with the Jewish High Holy Days, than for any games that they *did* play. "The true wholeness," wrote Rabbi Alter of Ger, "is when a person diminishes himself in order to be negated unto God."

Circumcision teaches us to surrender to God's will. It is, according to Bible scholar Aviva Gottlieb Zornberg, the model of how human feeling submits to God's will. Nothing but this desire to obey could explain such an obvious violation of parental feeling. Moreover, she writes, the father goes above and beyond the biblical command; he makes the circumcision ceremony even more joyful than God had originally commanded. "The father is so passionately concerned to 'do the will of his creator,' that, in effect, he begins to improvise," she writes.

Circumcision teaches that there are limits to everything. Men especially need to hear this. We do not single-handedly control everything. The world is not completely ours. A piece of us belongs to God. After all, when God revealed the Divine Self to Abram, God's Name is revealed as El Shaddai. El Shaddai can be translated as the God Who said, "*Dai!* Enough! There are limits to what you can do in your life!"

This is a very important God for men to meet.

And what shall we do with the argument that circumcision diminishes sexual pleasure and traumatizes young men? Sexual potency, while wonderful, isn't everything. The physician and moral theorist Leon Kass reminds us that Judaism sees virility and potency as less important than decency, righteousness, and holiness. According to the Bible, the father must remember (literally, "re-member") this, and by inflicting a wound upon his child's penis, he symbolically remakes his son's masculinity. By placing a mark on the penis, the father is saying that genital activity must be challenged, directed, and sanctified.

Let us not forget. There are consequences if the generations are deaf to the call of God. Hence, the call to Abraham: "**And if any male who is uncircumcised fails to circumcise the flesh of his foreskin, that person shall be cut off from his kin; he has broken My covenant. . . .**" (Genesis 17:14). As theologian Jacob Neusner puts it: "We see ourselves as God sees us: a family beyond time, joined by blood not of pedigree but circumcision . . . a genealogy framed by fifty generations of loyalty to the covenant in blood."

What a blessing! If only we can learn to see ourselves as God sees us!

today

i am

a man

Bar Mitzvah Reconsidered

I t is time for a major confession—I never had a bar mitzvah ceremony at the age of thirteen. The story is rather simple. My parents did something that I would never recommend Jewish parents doing: they didn't join a synagogue until I was already in the fifth grade. By then it was too late for me to enter the bar mitzvah track in our local religious school, which at the time was quite all right with me. I was somewhat timid about learning Hebrew, so I told my parents that I would rather concentrate on Jewish history and Bible study, which I loved. As a ten-year-old, I used to transform my elastic book strap into a sling shot, placing large rocks within it, pretending to be the young David. I would hurl those rocks at a large tree, which, for the afternoon, was playing the part of the Philistine giant Goliath.

True to the spirit of that era's Reform Judaism, my parents believed that the group ceremony of confirmation at the age of sixteen was more important than bar mitzvah. They correctly reasoned that thirteen years old was too young to truly understand the depth of Judaism. So confirmation became my Jewish goal.

This decision, not to have a bar mitzvah ceremony, aroused some controversy among my family and peers. As my thirteenth year approached, my friends and cousins went into the bar mitz-vah process. I remember that year as a dizzying carousel of parties at various restaurants, synagogue auditoriums, and catering halls, and how my cousins taunted me for not going through the bar mitzvah ceremony. "That means you'll never be a man!" they warned. Then came the subtle hints and suggestions from my great-aunts and great-uncles. "Don't you want to become bar mitzvah like your cousins?" The translation of that question was *not* "Don't you want to read Torah like your cousins?" It was more like "Don't you want a party and presents like your cousins?" The mother of one of my peers actually said to me, "Okay, so *don't* learn Hebrew. Do it from *transliteration* if you have to!" Translation: "Look, kid, don't mess around with this. If you let this rite of passage slip, who knows what might happen!"

The pressure worked. Six months before my thirteenth birth-day, I visited the rabbi at the synagogue. Mind you—that rabbi was never a huge public voice in the American Jewish community. Truth be told, he was a rather soft-spoken man, a lifelong bache-lor, a kind soul. I will always remember how he listened to me very carefully. "Yes," he said, "I suppose that we could get you 'quickie' tutoring in Hebrew. Of course, you would have to work with a tutor several times a week." Within a few minutes, he led me to understand that I wanted a party, not a rite of passage. Doing a "rush job" like that would "work," but not really. It would not have done anything for my connection to Judaism.

Within a year, my family left that synagogue to join another synagogue with a better youth program. I was confirmed at the new synagogue, graduated from Hebrew high school, became active in the youth group—and the rest is history. To this day, I remember my earlier rabbi with a special fondness—a fondness he earned for that precise moment in my young life. He could have acquiesced to my wishes. He could have created something that would have satisfied my momentary desires. But he didn't. He was no Abba Hillel Silver or Stephen S. Wise, thundering public voices of American Judaism. But at that moment, he demonstrated courage and standards. Whether he knew it or not, he taught me what it would mean to be a rabbi.

So I never had a bar mitzvah ceremony at the age of thirteen. Of course, I *was* bar mitzvah—"old enough to do mitzvot." Bar, and bat, mitzvah is what a young Jew automatically becomes at the age of thirteen, ceremony or no ceremony. I survived the taunting of my cousins and their suspicions that I would never become a true man. In fact, my cousins dropped out of religious school somewhere around the third stanza of the closing hymn *"Ein Keloheinu"* on the Sabbath mornings when they became bar mitzvah.

Some of my friends have even suggested that my several books on the subject of bar and bat mitzvah, *Putting God on the Guest List* and *For Kids—Putting God on Your Guest List*, are an overcompensation for this missing piece in my life. Some of them say that my inner child, or my inner adolescent, somehow needs a belated bar mitzvah ceremony. I don't think so. I have never really regretted missing that ritual.

I consoled myself with this important piece of information: I was not alone in lacking a bar mitzvah ceremony. None of the great Jews of antiquity—Abraham, Moses, David, Solomon, Rabbi Akiba—had bar mitzvah ceremonies. As a status, bar mitzvah comes into the Jewish world in the second century of the Common Era. The sage Judah ben Tema envisioned a life of Jewish study and responsibility: "At five, one should study Scripture; at ten, one should study Mishnah; at thirteen, one is ready to do mitzvot; at fifteen, one is ready to study Talmud; at eighteen, one is ready for the wedding canopy; at twenty, one is responsible for providing for a family" (Mishnah, *Avot* 5:24).

The most powerful references to the age of thirteen as a life passage come from the realm of Jewish lore. The story is, for me, the most powerful evocation of what it means to be a Jew in the world. It is the story of an incident in Abraham's childhood in Ur of the Chaldees. It tells how Abraham, the first Jew, actually became a Jew (*Genesis Rabbah* 38:13):

Abraham's family used to make idols and sell them in the market. One day, when it was Abraham's turn to sell, his father Terah gave him several baskets of household gods and set him up in the marketplace.

A man came to him and asked: Have you a god to sell? Abraham asked, "What kind of god do you wish to buy?" The man replied, "I am a mighty man—give me a god as mighty as I am!" So Abraham took an image that was standing on a shelf higher than all the others and said, "Pay the money and take this one. But first, a question. How old are you?" The man answered, "I am seventy years old." Abraham said: "Woe to a man who is seventy, yet would bow down before this thing which was made only today!" At that, the man flung the god back at Abraham and left the store.

Next came a widow, who said to Abraham: "I am a poor woman—give me a god as poor as I am." Abraham asked her, "How old are you?" "Quite old," she replied. Abraham then said: "To think that one so old would bow down before a god who is only one day old." She, too, left the store.

Then Abraham seized a stick, smashed all the idols, and placed the stick in the hand of the biggest of them. When his father returned, he asked: "Who did this to the gods?"

Abraham answered: "Would I hide anything from my father? A woman came with a bowl of fine flour and said, 'Here, offer it up to the gods.' When I offered it, the gods started fighting among themselves over who would eat it first. Then the biggest of them rose up and smashed all the others."

His father replied: "Are you making sport of me? They cannot do anything!"

Abraham answered: "You say they cannot. Let your ears hear what your mouth is saying!"

Here we have an ancient religious satire that pokes fun not only at idolatry, but at the religious and spiritual foibles of common, struggling people. The very absurdity of it—that Abraham's family used to make images and sell them in the market. Abraham's father, Terah, is in the idol business in Ur. In my imagination, he has a chain of designer idol boutiques in ancient Middle Eastern malls. It might even have been called "Gods R Us."

In the story, the young Abraham challenges his customers with the foolishness of worshiping something that was created only that day. This is the first critique of consumerism—the worship of the new and ephemeral. When Abraham smashes the idols, he performs the first act of iconoclasm. Breaking the false gods has always been the Jew's primary job description. With that act of breaking, Abraham shows that he is worthy to be called by God and to be a founder of a new people. This story is very popular. It is among the first stories that a Jewish child hears upon beginning religious school. But most people don't know that at the time, Abraham was thirteen years old. That was Abraham's proto–bar mitzvah ceremony.

Some years ago, I bought an ancient Sumerian idol from an

archaeologist in Jerusalem. It came from around 1800 B.C.E., Abraham's period. Now it stands on a shelf in my study. And when pre-bar and -bat mitzvah kids come in, I show them the idol and tell them the story. I tell them—and their parents—that challenging and questioning and the discovery of new truths is, in fact, the quintessential Jewish passage.

There are other Jewish texts about the importance of thirteen. At the age of thirteen, the twins Jacob and Esau went their separate ways: Jacob to the worship of God, Esau to idolatry. At that age, each "became" what they would ultimately be. Jacob's sons, Simeon and Levi, were thirteen when they retaliated against the people of Shechem after their sister, Dinah, was raped. Thirteen, then, is a time for moral fervor and learning what you should defend. The Talmud says that Bezalel, the "ancestor" of the famous art school in Jerusalem, was thirteen when he designed the ancient tabernacle in the wilderness. So thirteen is a time of great creativity as well—of harnessing our inner energies in order to design a place of holiness.

Classically, bar mitzvah was a time of great responsibility. Jews believed that the *yetzer ha-tov* (the good inclination) entered a boy at the time of bar mitzvah. A boy could now help constitute a minyan, the quorum of ten required for public worship. However, there was sadness as well. Fathers would utter a special prayer: *Baruch she-petarani me-onsho shel zeh:* "Blessed is the One who has now freed me from responsibility for this one." The father would no longer be responsible for his son's sins, though at least one scholar suggests that the child used to recite it about the father as well, as if to say, "And I am no longer responsible for my father, either." I once suggested that a child say that prayer as a way of understanding that he was not responsible for his father's public and well-known misbehaviors.

In Europe, bar mitzvah was a *comma*—a comma in the long, run-on sentence of Jewish life and responsibility. In America, it has become a *period*. The Old World bar mitzvah meant a real change in status, the attainment of religious maturity, the assumption of additional religious responsibilities. Bar mitzvah, as we know it, is an American Jewish invention. Bar mitzvah changed in America, and the changes have not been for the better.

Bar mitzvah should be much more than simply reading from the Torah, leading a service, giving a speech, having a party, and getting gifts. Bar mitzvah—and by extension, too much of Jewish education in this country—is no longer about Judaism or about responsibility. It has become about ritual performance. It is about what the prophet Isaiah called *mitzvat anashim u'melumdah*, a humanly required rite learned by rote. This is my principal observation and sadness about bar mitzvah and bat mitzvah in America: the guts have been taken out of it.

I have noticed an interesting gender issue in my work with young people becoming bar and bat mitzvah. When I ask Jewish boys about the meaning of bar mitzvah, they instinctively say, almost as if they had been programmed, "It's when I become a man." By contrast, when asked about the meaning of bat mitzvah, girls never say, "It's when I become a woman." My theory is that boys are socialized to look at incipient manhood as a time of privilege—learning to drive and being able to drink legally. If you consider the fact that the classic bar mitzvah gift was once the fountain pen, it begins to make some sense. Two generations ago, the fountain pen symbolized American corporate masculine privilege—the ability to endorse checks and sign contracts. Girls have a deeper sense of what it really means to become a woman, because there is a far deeper discussion among girls of the physical aspects of maturity. Moreover, even the way girls define maturity is different. When I ask boys about becoming bar mitzvah, they say, "It's when I get to do more stuff." Girls, however, speak about having more responsibilities as Jews.

As an active observer and participant in the ritual of bar mitzvah for more than twenty years, I have begun to sense that there has been a real disconnection between the rite of passage, and what that passage could potentially mean to the souls of Jewish boys. What does bar mitzvah need? Some years ago, the anthropologist Arnold Van Gennep conceptualized the basic adolescent initiation ritual. He saw the initiation ritual as a basic change in identity. The boy "dies," and the man is resurrected. Adolescence, therefore, is a time of second birth.

A self-confessed secular Israeli told me about his son's coming-of-age ceremony:

On my son's thirteenth birthday, I awakened my son at dawn. I had already packed a backpack with sandwiches, money, a flashlight, a knife, and a hatchet. My friends and I tied my son up, blindfolded him, put him in the back of our van, and drove him to the Negev. We then released him and told him: "Now find your way home." Three days later, he knocked on our door in Tel Aviv, threw his arms around me, and sobbed, "Thank you, Abba. I love you."

We are never quite as secular as we think. This so-called secular Israeli had, perhaps unconsciously, osmosed and combined two crucial stories from the book of Genesis—and he had acted them out upon his son!

The first story is the story of Hagar and Ishmael from the book of Genesis, which we discussed in chapter 2. Ishmael almost dies in the wilderness. Perhaps this is the seed of an ancient Near Eastern rite of passage. A boy is growing up. He is tested in the wilderness to see if he can survive. In this way, his childhood "dies," and his adulthood is "born."

There was a second story—the most famous Jewish story in the world. It is the story of the binding of Isaac, which we read in synagogue on Rosh Hashanah morning. God told Abraham to offer Isaac as a sacrifice on Mount Moriah, but an angel intervened to save the boy's life, and Abraham sacrificed a ram instead. Here, too, is the seed of an ancient rite of passage. Again, the ritual could have been the same. A father saw that his son was growing up. The father deliberately placed his son in danger, the boy almost died, and then was miraculously saved so that he could advance toward maturity.

One thing is certain. As Robert Bly writes, "Women can change the embryo to a boy, but only men can change the boy to a man. . . . Boys need a second birth, this time a birth from men." The father, or some other significant male presence in the young boy's life, must be involved in the passage in some way. The boy needs the father as a teaching presence in his life at that moment. Jewish law is very clear about the role of fathers: "A father is obligated to do these things for his son: circumcise him, redeem him [though the ritual of *pidyon ha-ben*, the redemption of the firstborn from the ancient duties of mandatory priesthood], teach him Torah, teach him a trade, find him a wife—and, some would say, teach him to swim." Jewish fathers have turned other men and women into our surrogates in those tasks. For some of them, modernity has simply rewritten and edited parental responsibility. But the boy needs the father or someone fatherlike for the passage into maturity.

Rethinking a Rite of Passage

A community educator named Stan Crow, quoted in Michael Gurian's book *A Fine Young Man*, has been creating and directing adolescent rites of passage in Seattle for many years. His philosophy is that newly emerging adolescents need mentors, ordeals, tests, rituals, and community celebration. What would the elements of such a passage be? How can we integrate them with the process of bar mitzvah and make them Jewish?

First, the boy should discard his old life in some way, in order to symbolize his rebirth. Newly emerging adolescent boys of the Maasai tribe in Africa have to give away childhood possessions. Jewish boys could give away or sell their old toys in a garage sale, using the proceeds for a charitable cause.

Over the years, I have heard many Jewish teenagers complain that, for them, Judaism itself has not changed. They want a grown-up version of Judaism, and not one that simply imitates and needlessly repeats the old patterns and content of previous religious training. I now use the bar and bat mitzvah age, and its immediate aftermath, to break some of the idols that our young people have been worshiping. I tell them that some of what they have learned in the past was appropriate for them as children, but that they are ready for some bigger truths, some examples being that Hanukkah is not about a jar of oil that lasted for eight nights, that there are racy and violent passages in the Bible, and that God will not always bail us out.

I would like to use the moment of bar mitzvah for kids to give some of their old and usable religious school textbooks to younger children. It could be done in a ritualized form, even at a public worship service. It could be a symbolic act for those young people, a way to say to themselves and to the community, "I have grown. The 'old me' has died. I am passing on my sources of earlier wisdom to another 'generation.'"

Second, I would like to see the youth create a set of questions that he wants answered by the elders of his community. The scholar of religion Mircea Eliade teaches that the puberty initiation represents the revelation of the sacred. In a primitive society, this does not only mean what we conventionally call "religion," but also an entire body of culture, tradition, and lore. That's how it used to be. In "the old days," Jewish boys became Jewish men under the tutelage and guidance of the older men in the community. Back then the elders of the community lived in our homes and right in our midst, not in Sun Belt retirement communities one thousand miles away. We turned to the elders for wisdom, knowledge, and informal tutoring in the skills of life. They could teach you how to *daven*, how to put on tefillin, how to cook a brisket, how to work on your marriage, or how to behave in the *shvitz*. Jewish education—life education—was less of a classroom affair and more of an active apprenticeship.

When I started my career back in Miami in the early 1980s, a young woman told me, "I would love to worship at your synagogue, but, frankly, there aren't enough old men there." "Sure there are," I responded, thinking of the rows of pews filled every Friday evening with retirees in white shoes and polyester jackets. "No," she said. "I know the kind of old men you are thinking of. I mean *old men*." She meant the old-time davening, putting-on-tefillin, "let's have a little shnaps after morning minyan" kind of guys.

A friend of mine once said, "We are missing the wisdom of old men in the Jewish community." I am beginning to agree. I have become haunted by this question: Has the American Jewish community become too rational and too professionalized? Is it possible to restore a sense of tribal wisdom to Jewish life? I believe that it is time for us to reacquaint the generations with each other. Older laymen (and not just rabbis, cantors, and educators) could teach Hebrew, Torah, and synagogue skills to younger boys in the community. Those men should be open and available for our youths to be able to ask them the questions of life and the questions of Jewish living and belief. The community could honor the elder-tutor at the bar mitzvah ceremony. Imagine how powerful this could be; imagine how this could help redeem and revive our fading concept of "community."

Third, the youth should prepare a solo trip in which he accepts that his boyhood is dying and that his manhood is emerging. Throughout religious history, the journey has been symbolic of maturation and change. Classically, it was the journey into and through the desert. Abraham journeys through the desert to come to the land of Israel. Moses journeys through the desert in order to begin his mission to save his people. In the Torah, the entire Jewish people crossed the desert so that the slave generation could die and a new, free generation could be born. The journalist Lincoln Steffens takes this to be the chief political lesson of the Exodus: "The grown-ups must die."

My first journey was not exactly solo, and it was not exactly through the desert. It was when I was only eight years old. My parents, with the encouragement of my grandmother, allowed me to go with some "older boys," all of eleven years old, to see the Mets play at the old Polo Grounds in upper Manhattan. This entailed taking the Long Island Railroad and a subway. It was, in many ways, a true rite of passage. As was the time my father let me drive on an expressway for the first time. As the dial moved up the speedometer, I heard my father sigh, for at that moment he could feel himself aging. I have a son who is old enough to drive fast, he must have been thinking.

The object of the journey is humility. I have been thinking about the meaning of a journey for my own son. Perhaps it will be to the Lower East Side or to the Museum of Jewish Heritage in lower Manhattan. Whatever it is, he will have to make his own lunch and bring it with him; call a cab or figure out how to get to the railroad station; find out when the trains run; take the train to New York City; navigate the subway system; and come back.

Sure, he's going to do it, but with my cell phone in his pocket!

Fourth, he must experience the life cycle in some way. Adolescent passage should mean that kids understand the flow of life better. For the first time in my career, and not too long ago, a young man who was preparing to become bar mitzvah became an older brother. He was present when his little brother was born, and he was present for the bris. I sense that his bar mitzvah experience was greatly enhanced by being there for the start of life as well as for his own passage. If I could, I would make sure that all thirteen-year-olds could be part of the entire range of life-cycle ceremonies. They need to understand how God's calendar works. I had this sort of experience with my own son. As part of his preparation for bar mitzvah, I sensed that my son—and other kids—had to be exposed to the life of mitzvah. So I decided to take him with me on some pastoral visits to hospitals. It was an important experience for him, because his fantasies of hospitals were all rooted in the *ER* television show. But more than this, he needed to see that nurture is a crucial piece of the male role.

Years ago, a close relative of my great-uncle Harry died. One evening during the shiva mourning period, the door to the house opened up and a group of people entered. Their holy task was to make the shiva minyan. Because mourners cannot leave the home during shiva, the community comes to pray with them. One of the visitors was a boy in his early teens. He went over to my great-uncle Harry and said to him: "May God console you on your loss." He then distributed prayer books to the mourners in the living room and began to lead the evening service. After the service was over, the boy went into the dining room, wrapped some rugelach in a napkin, shoved the little bundle into his pocket, returned to my great-uncle's side, shook the old man's hand, and left. I turned to my great-uncle and asked, "Who was that boy?" Uncle Harry shrugged his shoulders and answered, "A kid from the *shul* [synagogue]."

Such a beautiful gesture! The gesture said: "Who knows, and who cares?" Such beautiful words! "A kid from the *shul*." That was how Harry identified the boy—as part of his religious community. The boy had become bar mitzvah—old enough to do mitzvot. Someone in the synagogue—the rabbi, the cantor, the director of education, or a knowledgeable layperson—must have taken him aside and said, "Now that you are bar mitzvah, and old enough to do mitzvot, we're going to teach you the most delicate mitzvah imaginable. We're going to teach you how to go into a house of mourning and lead a service and walk mourners through the valley of the shadow of death." Now, *that's* Jewish education!

Fifth, there should be a physical challenge in some way. By and large, bar mitzvah is about intellectual preparation and the overcoming of performance jitters. It is very much in the head. There is a body piece as well. I once thought that the body piece of the Torah ritual was limited to the person who does *hagbah*, the lifting of the Torah scroll after it has been read, which serves as a dramatic evocation of the revelation at Sinai. Someone pointed out to me that bar and bat mitzvah kids also see a physicality to it all. In our synagogue, the children carry the scroll and place it back inside the Holy Ark. The children see that act of physically carrying the Torah as a moment of passage as well.

All of which got me to thinking: Should there be other physical adventures in bar mitzvah? For example, might bar mitzvah training include Jewish "Outward Bound" camping programs for bar mitzvah candidates? A Reform rabbi named Niles Goldstein is a Torah teacher and part-time adventurer. He has helped create a venture called Jewish Adventure Travel, "where the call of the wild meets the call of faith." He proposes the creation of father-son outings, such as camping trips, rock climbing, or bicycle trips as part of the bar mitzvah process. Each trip would create a mini-community with mentors and father figures. In addition, it would feature a rabbi-in-residence and a curriculum. The curriculum would include such topics for discussion, such as, "What does Judaism say about overcoming obstacles?" "What does Judaism teach us about confronting and overcoming our fears?" or "What does Judaism teach about teamwork and interdependence?"

Why boys? Certainly girls and mothers would be welcome and encouraged to come, but why an emphasis on boys? Because America was founded, and continues to exist, on the myth of the rugged individual. John Wayne is our hero. So is Rick Blaine of *Casablanca:* "I stick my neck out for nobody." But the rugged individual has become a broken myth. We *do* need other people. Boys in particular need to know that they need others and that they may express emotions. Boys need to hear the sages' advice: "Do not separate yourself from the community."

Perhaps an issue of even more concern: The controversies in contemporary liberal Judaism are all about the body, not about the mind. Jews worry, Should rabbis perform wedding ceremonies that sanctify Jewish bodies uniting with non-Jewish bodies? Should rabbis perform ceremonies that sanctify male bodies uniting with male bodies, and female bodies uniting with female bodies? Is there any religious significance to kashrut—to what we do put and don't put into our bodies? Should we encourage liberal Jews to put tefillin on their liberal Jewish arms, or yarmulkes on their liberal Jewish heads, or *tallitot* (prayer shawls) around their liberal Jewish shoulders? The Jewish people has been disembodied in the Diaspora, and it has looked to Israel for embodiment— for examples of Jews who use their bodies to build the Jewish people. The active, physical body must return to Jewish life.

Sixth, there should be an artistic challenge. The boy must create something. Stan Crow suggests that the creation be placed on an altar in the boy's room. Even more Jewish, the boy should create something that is presented on the "altar" of the synagogue. In most cases, this is the *dvar Torah*, the sermonette on the Torah portion that young Jews deliver when they become bar or bat mitzvah. The creation of that text should be seen as an essential part of emerging adulthood.

Seventh, there should be a communal celebration—which is to say there should be a community. Crow reminds us that adolescent boys need clans to help them make the transition. The clan consists of father, mother, grandparents, uncles, aunts, older friends, mentors, coaches, teachers, friends, legendary figures, and departed relatives. As Michael Gurian wrote in *A Fine Young Man*, "If a boy has no real clan in place before he enters adolescence, he's very likely to go out and find one that consumes him, tribalizes him, redirects him, even brainwashes him—a formal gang, a peer group that disaffects him, a cult, a media obsession."

A young Jew-by-choice told me how he had become a man back in northern Wisconsin. It happened on the day when he was allowed for the first time to hunt with the "big boys" and the older men. They solemnly took it upon themselves to show him how to hold the rifle and how to find the game. Unlike the way modern Jews deal with bar mitzvah, in this rite of passage the older men did not delegate their tasks to a professional hunting teacher. They taught the young man themselves, which reinforced to them what this passage and what this kind of knowledge and skill really meant.

There is something here in the great folk love of bar mitzvah. The bar and bat mitzvah experience certainly feels like a trial. A young person is growing up. The child struggles with learning Torah and then has to present it to a community. I experienced this recently in the synagogue. The bar mitzvah boy was chanting the blessings for the scriptural portion that he would be reading. In the congregation, however, his friends were singing along with him. At first, I didn't know how to feel about it. After all, they were potentially stepping on his lines and upstaging him. Then I realized that I had fallen prey to a mind-set that I have been combating for years—this notion that the bar and bat mitzvah ceremony is a performance, a sort of sacred recital in which the congregation should remain dutifully silent. No, I said to myself, there was something delightful in the young man's peers singing along with him. It was their way of saying, "Hey, we're all in this together. Some of us have already chanted that blessing and some of us have yet to sing that blessing. But it is our 'song' of Jewish maturity." In a time when true religious community is hard to find, it was tribal!

Finally, there needs to be a process of preparation. Preparation is not only Torah and prayer; it must encompass something deeper as well.

We teach, long and hard, about how bar mitzvah is a covenantal ceremony that renews the emerging Jewish adult's connection to Torah. What do Jewish boys really need to know in order to be Jewish men? They certainly are not learning it now. If the nature of American Jewish celebration is any clue, then it is fair to say that they are learning the wrong messages about adulthood—messages about conspicuous consumption. Or worse. At a Long Island bar mitzvah party, there were pictures of scantily clad women on the walls of the social hall. The bar mitzvah boy entered the party on a chariot that was pulled by four women in bikinis. The theme of the party was *Playboy*. I don't know what the parents had in mind, but the lesson that the boy learned about desires, women, and the roles of the sexes will stay with him even beyond the day when they will have finished paying off the bills for the celebration. Emerging Jewish men need to know how to treat women and how to deal with temptations, anger, violence, and ambition. Perhaps that should be the curriculum for bar mitzvah in the next century.

We must transform the bar mitzvah process into one in which we discuss the real ethical and spiritual implications of Jewish manhood.

The Wisdom of Jewish Men

Nowadays we read the texts of the rabbinic sages through different sets of eyes. When we see the word *man* or *men*, we tend to translate that term in a non–gender specific way. We assume that the words of the sages are often addressed to all people, not just to one gender. I accept that change. And yet this linguistic transformation cannot negate that the sages who created rabbinic Judaism were, in the words of my teacher Lawrence Hoffman, "an old boys' club." Even the Jewish family of fable and lore is a relatively modern construction. The famed Passover seder at B'nei Brak, discussed in the classic Haggadah text, was a "men only" seder—and they probably used the opportunity to speak encoded language about a rebellion against the Romans. When the sages used terms like *ish* or *adam*, meaning "man" or "men," they probably *meant* precisely that—"men." They tended to see women as Other, requiring special rules, regulations, borders, and boundaries.

Without attempting to turn back the clock on our modern sense of egalitarianism, I have looked at a selection of texts and sayings that contain advice addressed to *men* in particular. I was looking to see what they might say about Jewish manhood, and I found that it is time to start looking at these texts again. Various studies show that Jewish male teenagers demonstrate less commitment to their Jewish identity than do their female counterparts. Perhaps Jewish boys need to hear how our holy, ancient words can speak to them once again.

Be Principled, But Flexible

Once a heathen was passing by a synagogue and heard the Torah's description of the garments of the High Priest. The heathen said to himself: "I will go and convert to Judaism so that I may be appointed the high priest of the Temple in Jerusalem." He went before the sage Shammai and said to him, "Convert me so that I can become the high priest." Shammai promptly drove him away, threatening him with a builder's ruler in his hand.

When the heathen went before the sage Hillel, Hillel converted him to Judaism, but then he told the convert, "A king is not appointed unless he knows the details of how to rule. You must go now and study the details of how the Temple is run!"

The convert went and read Scripture. He came to the verse "The outsider [anyone who is not a Levite and is not supposed to be involved in the work of the Tabernacle] that comes near the Tabernacle [the ancient version of the Temple in Jerusalem] shall be put to death" (Numbers 1:51). He asked Hillel, "To whom does this verse apply?" Hillel replied: "Even to someone as great as David, who was the king of Israel."

At that, the convert said to himself: "If that applies to someone as great as King David, and if it applies to someone who is not a priest, and someone who is a born Jew, what hope is there for me to be the High Priest?"

So he went to Shammai and asked him, "How could I ever have thought that I would be eligible to become the High Priest? Is it not written in the Torah, 'The outsider that comes near the Tabernacle shall be put to death'?"

He then went before Hillel and said to him, "Oh, gentle Hillel, may blessings rest on your head for bringing me under the wings of the Divine Presence!"

Some time later, the new Jew thought about this and he said to himself, "Shammai's harshness nearly drove me away, but Hillel's gentleness brought me under the wings of the Divine Presence." For that reason the sages say: A man should always be as flexible as Hillel, not as inflexible as Shammai (Talmud, *Shabbat* 31a).

Commentary: Shammai would have nothing to do with this man. He even used physical violence to drive him away. On the one hand, who would blame him? After all, the man was interested in becoming a Jew only because he wanted the most important job in the Jewish world—to be the High Priest at the Temple in Jerusalem. On the other hand, Hillel, who is always Shammai's rival in matters of Jewish law and practice, promptly accepted the potential convert to Judaism. Hillel didn't care that the man only seemed to want glory for himself. Hillel reasoned: "So let him want to be the High Priest! As long as this is what he wants, he has to learn Judaism on the way to getting there." The man's studies showed him that his goal of being the High Priest would not work out, because of the severe consequences of approaching the sanctuary if one is not supposed to be working there. Yes, he was disappointed— but he became a learned Jew even as he learned about his own limitations.

Shammai was wrong for driving the man away. Hillel was right for welcoming him into the Jewish people and for treating him like an intelligent person. Shammai thought that he was losing a gentile who only had ego needs. Hillel saw a good Jew within the man who had ego needs. The lesson for young men is that it is good to have strong principles like Shammai. But you should also be able to see the bigger and deeper picture, and therefore be as flexible as Hillel.

Living in Community

Rabban Yochanan ben Zakkai said: Go into the world and observe the right course a man should steadfastly follow.

Rabbi Eliezer said: Be generous with your means.

Rabbi Joshua said: Be a good friend.

Rabbi Yose said: Be a good neighbor.

Rabbi Simeon said: Consider the consequences of your actions.

Rabbi Eleazar said: Cultivate an unselfish heart (Mishnah, Avot 2:10–11, 13).

Commentary: To be a mature man is to know that you live in the midst of a community. That means several things. First, maturity demands generosity. Rabbi Eliezer suggests that you give freely of what you have. Apparently it is not enough to simply give freely. According to Rabbi Eleazar, you have to feel it in your heart as well. To be a mature man, you also have to be a good friend and be a good neighbor. The two are not necessarily the same thing. Being a good friend implies an emotional attachment to people; being a good neighbor implies knowing the rules of citizenship and what it means to live in a society in which people are connected to each other. For that reason, you have to know that what you do has consequences, and you must think about what those consequences are before you act. This not only applies to living in community—it also applies to what you do within your own life.

Passing the Tests of Manhood

By three things is a man tested:

By the way he does business

By the amount of wine he drinks

By the length of his talk (*Avot deRabbi Nathan 31*).

Commentary: The greatest temptations of manhood exist within the realm of business. We are tempted to treat others like objects of our desires; to look at the world as if it were "a jungle out there," and therefore behave like animals; to cut corners; to cheat; and to mistreat workers. "Brazenness, rather than moral sensitivity," said the contemporary Jewish theologian Professor Eugene B. Borowitz, is often trumpeted as the sign of a competent executive."

There is a kosher way to drink—in moderation, and not for the purpose of getting drunk. A man is known by the way he manages his cup, the way he deals with consuming. It is a metaphor for the entire realm of the appetite—whether it is food, or drink, or sex, for that matter. Living in moderation, living as a combination of the angelic and the earthly, is all that God can want of us.

There are many Jewish teachings about speech. But here we learn one thing—be careful how much you say. Do you know why the tongue is surrounded by walls of flesh and a cage of teeth? Because it is that dangerous.

Being a Man

Hillel said: In a place where there are no men, strive to be a man (*hishtadeyl lihiyot ish*) (Mishnah, Avot 2:6).

Commentary: Here we can jump around the biblical text, looking at different instances of the word *ish*, "man." From this little journey through the text, we might actually get a clue as to what it means to be a man.

Jacob wrestled with a man (*ish*) in the middle of the night. We don't know the true identity of the assailant, but one version of being a man is being the one who challenges another to struggle and to grow.

When Joseph was lost in the fields, looking for his brothers, a certain man (*ish*) found him, and directed him toward his brothers. He is also a nameless man, though there are some traditions that say he was the angel Gabriel. Gabriel had been sent into that moment in history to reconnect Joseph with his brothers. Because of him, Joseph found his brothers, was sold into slavery by them, went down into Egypt, gained power in Egypt, saved Egypt from famine, met his brothers again, invited them to settle in Egypt . . . which brings Jewish people into Egypt . . . which gets us out of Egypt, and to Sinai, and into the wilderness, and . . . And so we see, that each of us can become *ish*, a man who is capable of doing some small thing that moves history forward.

Finally, we come to the moment in Moses' life when he realizes that he is a Hebrew (Exodus 2: 11-12).

204 SEARCHING FOR MY BROTHERS

Some time after that, when Moses had grown up, he went out to his kinsfolk, and witnessed their labors. He saw an Egyptian beating a Hebrew, one of his kinsmen. He turned this way and that, and, seeing no one (*ish*), he struck down the Egyptian and hid him in the sand.

Why did the privileged Moses kill the Egyptian? And who was he looking for before he did so? It's not that he was looking to see if anyone would spy him committing this act of heroism. Moses was looking to see if there was anyone else there to help. Moses was looking to see if there was anyone else there to intervene. Moses was looking for a *real man*. That is the true impact of Hillel's statement. When there is no one else around to act courageously, do it. That is not only what it means to be a *man;* it is also what it means to be a *mensch*.

How to Speak

The sages in the school of Rabbi Ishmael taught: A man should always use refined speech, because it is written: "That which my lips know they shall speak in purity" (Job 33:3) (Talmud, *Pesachim* 3a).

Rabbi Simeon ben Yohai said: A man should speak of his superiority with a soft voice and of his shortcomings with a loud voice.

Of his superiority with a soft voice, as may be seen in the confession at tithing (Deuteronomy 26:13): "Then you shall say before the Lord your God, I have brought away the hallowed things out of my house, and also have given them to the Levite, and to the stranger, to the orphan, and to the widow, according to all your commandments which you have commanded me; I have not transgressed your command-ments, nor have I forgotten them."

Of his shortcomings in a loud voice, as may be seen in the confession at the bringing of first fruits: "A wandering Aramean was my father and he went down into Egypt, and sojourned there with a few, and became there a nation, great, mighty, and populous. And the Egyptians dealt ill with us, and afflicted us, and laid upon us hard slavery. And when we cried to the Lord God of our fathers, the Lord heard our voice, and looked on our affliction, and our labor, and our oppression. And the Lord brought us out of Egypt with a mighty hand, and with an outstretched arm, and with great awesomeness, and with signs, and with wonders' " (Deuteronomy 26:5) (Talmud, *Sotah* 32b).

A wise man does not speak before one who is greater than he in wisdom, does not break in on the words of his fellow, is not hasty to answer, asks what is relevant and answers what is appropriate, speaks on the first point first and on the last point last, says of that which he has not heard: "I have not heard it," and acknowledges the truth (*Avot* 5:7).

Commentary: There is a kosher way to speak in this world, and in order to be a real man, men should know it. Rabbi Judah Loewe of Prague was the creator of the Golem, the famous Jewish Franken-stein monster who protected the Jews from their enemies. He created the golem by using the Name of God. Rabbi Loewe taught: "The Hebrew word for language, *lashon,* is a great word. The first letter, *lamed,* points upward —to remind us that our language can bring us to the heavens. But the last letter, *nun,* points downward—to remind us that our language can plunge us into the abyss."

Refined speech means not using obscenity. Men should also speak with humility. When it is time to speak of something that you have done well, downplay it. On the other hand, when it is time to speak of something that you have not done so well, emphasize it. Here the Torah's example is the traditional declaration that an Israelite made at the ancient Temple upon presenting the tithing of the first fruits. When speaking of the charity that he/she has done, the declaration is made with a soft voice. But when speaking of one's humble origins ("My father was a wandering Aramean, etc."), you speak in a loud voice.

The rest seems like basic etiquette. I especially love the line about admitting that you don't know something. This virtue is sorely lacking nowadays. I once heard Professor Eugene Borowitz respond to a question in a public lecture. Someone asked him, "Why can't we say the unpronounceable four-letter Name of God if we think we know how to pronounce it?" I will never forget Dr. Borowitz's rapier-like response: "Because we don't have to say everything we think we know."

Self Control

Happy is the man who, hearing himself abused, remains silent. He thereby wards off a hundred evils from himself (Talmud, *Sanhedrin* 7a).

Commentary: How hard is it to restrain oneself from striking back when verbally abused? Someone once asked the Nobel laureate Elie Wiesel, "Is there a tradition of silence in Judaism?" "Yes, there is," he replied, "but no one talks about it."

This is why I love the words that are traditionally assigned to the silent meditation in Jewish liturgy: "O Lord, keep my tongue from evil, and my lips from speaking deceitfully. To those who curse me, let my soul be silent, and let my soul be like dust to everyone." The nineteenth-century Rabbi Hayyim ben Isaac, the founder of the famed *yeshiva* in Volozhin, said that we should ignore insults because the less we care about our prestige, the less we will allow our selfishness to get in the way of serving God and improving ourselves.

Here is yet another difference between Jewish ethics and the ethics of the contemporary world. Jewish macho is to learn to be quiet when people are disrespecting you. Imagine saying to yourself when people are giving you a rough time, "Well, that's their problem." This is as close as Judaism comes to a general philosophy of pacifism. Yes, Jews will defend their land and their rights, but their egos—this is another thing altogether. In Hasidic thinking, there is an idea called *bittul ha-yesh*, "the annihilation of selfhood," in which the self and its needs disappear into the very cosmos. This is very difficult. It is more than a sign of macho. It is a sign of self-control.

How To Reprove

Rabbi Judah the Patriarch said: What is the right way a man should choose for himself?

He should love reproofs. As long as there are reproofs in the world, peace of mind comes to the world, good and blessing come to the world, and evil departs from the world, as is said, "But to them that are eager to be reproved, there shall come delight, and the blessing of good shall come upon them" (Proverbs 24:25) (Talmud, *Tamid* 28a).

Commentary: The biblical source for the duty to rebuke the wrongdoer is, **"You shall not hate your kinsman in your heart. Reprove your neighbor, but incur no guilt because of him"** (Leviticus 19:17). Some sages believed that the Second Temple was destroyed because the righteous did not fulfill their obligation to rebuke the wrongdoers of their time, and thus shared their guilt (Talmud, *Shabbat* 119b). However, there are limits. You should criticize people in private, if you can, because embarrassing someone in public is tantamount to shedding blood.

How to Manage Your Emotions

Resh Lakish said: When a man becomes angry—if he is a sage, his wisdom departs from him; if he is a prophet, his prophecy departs from him (Talmud, *Pesachim* 66b).

Commentary: Male anger is pure testosterone, says Michael Gurian. Elsewhere in rabbinic teachings, we are told not to try to placate someone at the moment of their anger. Gurian would agree; sometimes you just have to ride it out with someone who is angry, or let it pass.

Anger handled irresponsibly can be devastating. The sages noticed that anger can relieve a person of his better judgment. A prophet can even lose his God-given ability to prophesy. Jews in particular must ask, "What are we angry about? How much anger do we carry within us, still—about the Holocaust, about anti-Semitism, about the torments of Jewish history? Have we allowed that anger to stunt us emotionally? Have we permitted that anger to blind us to the fact that not everyone in the world hates us, or has ever hated us? Has our anger caused the spirit of wisdom and prophecy to depart from us?" We should choose the targets and subjects of our anger with wisdom and with care. We should learn how to control our tempers, realizing that blowing off steam may feel great at the moment but can have lasting effects. Consider the devastating, murderous act of violence in Littleton, Colorado—adolescent male anger at its most horrific.

A Man's Body

Rabbi Levi said: Six organs serve man—three are under his control, and three are not under his control.

The eyes, the ears, and the nose are not under his control: he sees what he does not wish to see; he hears what he does not wish to hear; and he smells what he does not wish to smell.

The mouth, the hands, and the feet are under his control: the mouth, if he wishes, will occupy itself with Torah or, if he prefers, slander, revile, and blaspheme. The hands, if he wishes, will distribute charity or, if he prefers, steal and slay. The feet, if he wishes, will walk to synagogues and houses of study or, if he prefers, walk to theaters and circuses [which the sages considered idolatrous and frivolous places] (*Genesis Rabbah* 67:3).

Commentary: I love this text, because it helps define both social responsibility and personal freedom in Judaism. We do see, hear, and smell things that we don't wish to encounter. True, we can cover our eyes, plug our ears, and hold our noses—but there are sights, sounds, and stenches in the world of which we need to be aware. Those three senses conjure up the non-Jews who lived in the vicinities of the concentration camps. Surely they saw, heard, and smelled things. Many turned aside. Those who refused to do so were often heroes.

Then the text segues into a discussion of free will in Judaism. It basically says that the mouth, hands, and feet are ethically neutral, and totally within our control. We choose how to use them—whether to put them to holy uses or whether to degrade them by our actions.

The Management of Desires

Rabbi Yudan said in the name of Rabbi Aibu: No man departs from the world with even half his desire gratified. If he has one hundred, he wants to turn it into two hundred, and if he has two hundred, he wants to turn it into four hundred (*Ecclesiastes Rabbah* 1:13).

Commentary: The text speaks of the utter insatiability of man's desire. The text expresses this in financial terms, but it is true of other desires as well—fame, sex, things. That seems to be the way things are.

And yet I remember a story about the late Senator Paul Tsongas of Massachusetts. Shortly after he was diagnosed with cancer, he was walking on a Washington sidewalk with his daughter. Suddenly a biker pulled up on a Harley-Davidson. The biker had a long, flowing beard and his visible skin was covered with tattoos.

"Hey!" he yelled at Tsongas. "She's better!"

Tsongas, puzzled, asked, "Better than what?"

"Better than a Senate career!" the biker yelled, and with a wave, sped off.

"our father, our king"

A Male God Is Not as Bad as You Think

1 was once speaking with a father whose daughter had become bat mitzvah in our synagogue. It was several weeks after the ceremony. "So, how are you doing in these post-bat mitzvah days?" I asked jovially.

The father said, "I'm really glad we hired that guy to videotape the bat mitzvah ceremony. I watch that tape often. Whenever I get thoroughly fed up with my daughter, that's when I put it on."

I said to the proud father, "That's what God does as well. Every year, by the time Rosh Hashanah comes around, God is feeling fed up with the Jewish people. And then God hears us reading the story of the *Akedah*, the binding of Isaac, in the synagogue on Rosh Hashanah morning. It's like God is watching the video of that story. Then God hears the blowing of the shofar, the ram's horn. God remembers that Abraham was ready to offer his beloved son as a sacrifice. God says, 'Abraham would have done that? Oh, all right. I'll cut his descendants just a little more slack this year.'"

The father laughed at my theological reflection. He had just seen his own fatherhood as a reflection of the fatherhood of God. At that moment, he understood how the experience of being a father and being God are, in fact, interrelated. At that moment he came to realize that fatherhood is a metaphor for God, and vice versa.

As I walked away from that encounter, I thought about my own experiences as a father. We can never totally know God. The only glimpse we can have of God's inner life is thinking about what it's like to be a parent. You watch your infant roll over for the first time. You coax her to do it, cheering her on, wondering if you should help or not, wondering if she will get it on her own. That's the way it is with God and humanity as well. God creates the world, but the very next act of creation in the Bible—the building of Noah's ark—is left up to Noah himself. God might give the instructions, but Noah—and all humanity—has to start working on his own.

Then your child starts to walk. You are terrified that he may fall and that he may get hurt. You can put gates on the stairways so he doesn't tumble down the steps, but you know that the world just isn't constructed that way. You must step back and let your child fall. It's the only way he will grow. That's the way it is with God and humanity as well. Some of us may want a perfectly ordered world in which people cannot hurt or do evil. But such a world, though idyllic, robs humanity of its freedom. It is too big a price for us, and even God, to pay.

You entertain your child with a game of peekaboo. "Here I am . . . oops, I'm gone . . . I'm back again." Your child smiles at your presence, gets worried about your absence, and laughs in delight when she sees you again. That's the way it is with God and humanity as well. Several times in the Torah, God threatens to hide the Divine Face from us. The prophet Isaiah said: "For a small moment I have forsaken you; but with a great love I will gather you back. In wrath I hid my face from you for a moment;

but with everlasting kindness I will have compassion on you." But then God removes His hands from His face and His children can see who He is. At that moment, there is supernal delight as well.

Is God Male?

Let's get it right. God is beyond gender. But throughout history, when Jews conceived of a personal God, God most often turned out to be male. On the Days of Awe (Rosh Hashanah and Yom Kippur) when most Jews "visit" God, God is *Avinu malkeinu*— "Our Father, Our King." In Yiddish, God is *tatte*, "Papa." In the Sabbath morning hymn, *Anim Zemirot*, the poet says that God is beyond all allegories and beyond all pictures. And yet "They envisioned in You agedness and virility, and the hair of Your head as hoary and jet black. Aged on judgment day and virile on the day of battle, like a man of war whose powers are many." When God fought for the Jews, like at the crossing of the Red Sea, God was like a virile young man. But on Yom Kippur, when God is a judge, God is like an old man filled with compassion.

Many people of faith find male-dominated God language increasingly problematic. Jewish feminism has not only been about securing equal liturgical roles for women. Nor has it only been about moving Jewish women into the leadership positions they deserve. The feminist interpretation of religion has led to the questioning of the patriarchal God. Both Jewish and Christian feminists question the idea of a male God who controls everything: the transcendent God who is found at the top of heights, and surely the God who rules by decree. Their logic is impeccable. As the Christian feminist Mary Daly wrote in *Beyond God the Father:* "If God in his heaven is a father ruling his people, then it is in the nature of things and according to the divine play and the order of the universe that society be male-dominated."

Others believe that this notion of God as male is merely the product of the limitations of language, for Hebrew lacks a neuter gender. To refer to God as "He" is preferable, some say, to referring to God as "It" or to the linguistic barbarity of dispensing with pronouns altogether. Some prefer that we start using feminine terms for God in worship. There are, indeed, feminine images of God in Judaism, such as Shechinah, the Wandering Indwelling Feminine Presence of God.

Some feminists suggest a reclamation of the ancient pre-Israelite notion of the goddess. Here radical feminism walks hand in hand with an interpretation of history that portrays Judaism as a patriarchal society. Some scholars suggest that the Israelite invasion of Canaan was a deliberate attempt to destroy a matriarchal, goddess-based Canaanite religion. The mythologist Joseph Campbell traced the beginning of Western civilization to the great river valleys: the Nile, the Tigris-Euphrates, the Indus, and later the Ganges. That was the world of the Goddess. Then came waves of invasions in the fourth millennium B.C.E. These invaders were herders of cattle, former hunters whose bloodlust was unabated. They brought in warrior gods like Zeus or Yahweh and annihilated the primordial mother gods. He writes: "The Hebrews were absolutely ruthless in regard to their neighbors. . . . When the Hebrews came in, they really wiped out the Goddess."

To my ears, this sounds frightfully close to classic anti-Semitism. Once upon a time, Jews were Christ-killers. Now, in the minds of some of the academic elite, Jews have become Goddess-killers as well.

Feminist scholars such as Tikva Frymer-Kensky *(In the Wake of the Goddesses)* have resurrected some very crucial scholarship about ancient goddesses. Such scholarship is absolutely crucial in order that we have a fuller understanding of the roots of our civilization and the theological underpinnings that inform it. However, the fabled goddess of antiquity was not always such a bargain. As Cynthia Ozick notes, "What? Millennia after the cleansing purity of Abraham's vision of the One Creator, a return to Astarte, Hera, Juno, Venus, and all their proliferating sisterhood? Sex goddesses, fertility goddesses, mother goddesses? The sacrifices brought to these were often enough human. This is the new vision intended to 'restore dignity' to Jewish women?"

The Father God Isn't So Bad

If God can no longer be masculine, then it stands to reason that God can no longer be a Father. Why should God have it any easier than the rest of us? As Ken Woodward wrote in *The New York Times:* "These are tough times to be a father. The media are full of stories about abusive fathers, fatherless children, and deadbeat dads—and about New Fathers who are trying to do better. But in general this is an age when fathers get little respect, and you don't have to look farther than the biggest father figure of them all, God. Few theologians these days seem to want a God who takes charge, assumes responsibility, fights for his children, makes demands, risks rebuffs, punishes as well as forgives. In a word, a Father."

It is not my intention to disregard feminist theology. Not by a long shot. Religious feminists rightfully resent exclusively male God language. If God is to be more than a mere Idea, then we need a relationship with that God. True, there are many metaphors for that human-divine relationship. The liturgy of the Jewish High Holy Days contains the richest catalog of such metaphors: God is a Father; we are His children. God is a vine keeper; we are His vineyard. We are God's beloved; He is our friend. The holy of holies of relationships is the parental relationship, and a generic parent simply doesn't exist. Ask any child that. When your daughter stubs her toe, she does not run into the house yelling, "Parent! Parent!"

To paraphrase Oscar Wilde: When we are young we idealize our parents; when we are adolescents we judge them; when we are older we understand them. The same is true of our relationship with God as Father. When the Jews were a young people, they idealized the God who redeemed them from Egypt and gave them Torah. In the Jewish adolescence, which began with the destruction of Judean independence in 70 C.E. and ended with the Shoah, Jews began to judge the God who no longer spoke, who seemed not to hear prayers, who seemed helpless, who seemed to have abandoned His people. Now that the Jewish people is older, Jews can understand that God may not be all-powerful, just as our parents are not all-powerful, and God needs us as much as we need God. We can understand that the imagery with which we approach the Divine is much richer than we had imagined.

A FATHER GOD TEACHES MEN
HOW TO BE BETTER FATHERS

The image of God as father can actually teach men about fatherhood. As Rabbi Laura Geller said: "There is something in my relationship with my father that opens me up to God and there is something about my encounter with God that opens me up to my father."

There have been times when my father and I have been angry with each other, especially in my adulthood. These have been painful stretches of anger that seem endless because the animosity is filled with silence. It is the same with God and humanity. Does God's long silence since the end of divine revelation in the Torah stem from disgruntlement? Or might it be because we have not taken the time to hear what God is saying? When my father and I fought and made up, I understood the true meaning of repentance. It has served as a living theological laboratory that teaches not only about repairing the relationship with a parent, but in some way, with God as well.

Just as there is God-hunger in many of us, there is father-hunger as well. Rabbi Arnold Jacob Wolf, a Reform rabbi from Chicago, writes poignantly: "My father died when I was seven years old and from then on I needed desparately to find a Father who would not die." Moreover, the Father God of the Jewish tradition is not an oppressive father figure. Rabbi Richard Levy writes in his High Holy Day prayer book: "How would you like your mother to be? How would you like your father to be? Your parents have the potential to be that way, but God is that way now." The fatherly aspect of God is one of firmness and fairness, active when necessary and compassionate when desirable. It means the creative combination of both distance and intimacy, of the urge to love and the need to control.

In Hasidic tales, God often appears as King/Father and Israel appears as a son. A popular motif is the estrangement between the generations, which is a metaphor for the estrangement between God and Israel. Even when there is tension, closeness and love break the tension.

Once a king's son sinned against his father, the king. His father expelled him from his house. As long as he was near his home, people knew he was a king's son, and befriended him, and gave him food and drink. But as the days passed, and he got farther into his father's realm, no one knew him, and he had nothing to eat. He began to sell his clothing to buy food. When he had nothing left to sell, he hired out as a shepherd. After he had hired out as a shepherd he was no longer in need, because he needed nothing. He would sit on the hills, tending his flocks and singing like the other shepherds, and he forgot that he was a king's son and all the pleasures that he had been used to.

Now it is the custom of the shepherds to make themselves small roofs of straw to keep out the rain. The king's son wanted to make himself a roof, too, but he could not afford one, so he was deeply grieved.

Once the king happened to be passing through that province. Now it was a common practice in that kingdom for those who had petitions to write out their petitions and throw them into the king's chariot. The king's son came with the other petitioners, and threw his note, in which he petitioned for a straw roof such as shepherds have. The king recognized his son's handwriting and was saddened to think how low his son had fallen that he had forgotten that he was a king's son, and felt only the lack of a straw roof.

The Jews, too, had forgotten that they were royal children. But their messages in the form of heartfelt prayers can reach God, and God remembers who they are, even if they don't quite remember.

A story is told in the name of the Hasidic rebbe, Simcha Bunem of Pshischke:

A prince rebelled against his father and was consequently exiled. Many days later, his father's compassion was aroused, and the king sent a messenger to look for his son. After much searching, the messenger found him, dressed in rags, dancing in a pub in a distant city. He was dancing among many drunk people, from among the poorest of the populace.

The minister bowed before the prince and said to him: "I have been sent by your father, my lord the king, to ask of you, 'What is your desire, and what is your request?' The king's son burst into tears and said, "If it please my father the king, let him order that I be given sturdy boots, shining and gleaming."

The Rebbe concluded: "So it is too with us. When we pray to our Father in Heaven, we bring puny requests, for food and livelihood, but we do not cry out about the exile of the Shechinah [the Divine Presence] nor do we request complete redemption. The greatest sin of a Jew is that he forgets that he is the son of a King."

God Can Be Wrong—and Loves It

God can change his mind—like a good father. The Bible teaches that God regretted the Flood that wiped out humanity. When the Israelites sinned by creating a Golden Calf, God was ready to destroy the Jewish people. Moses intervened with Him, and He repented of His destructive desire.

God not only changes His mind. God can even be wrong. The Talmud records a famous incident in which a group of sages were debating whether or not a certain oven was ritually clean and therefore appropriate for use (Baba Metzia 59b):

On that day Rabbi Eliezer brought forward every imaginable argument, but the sages did not accept any of them. Finally he said to them, "If the *halacha* [Jewish law] agrees with me, let this carob tree prove it!"

The carob tree was uprooted and replanted a hundred cubits away from its place. "No proof can be brought from a carob tree," they retorted.

Again he said to them, "If the *halacha* agrees with me, let the channel of water prove it!" Sure enough, the channel of water flowed backward. "No proof can be brought from a channel of water," they rejoined.

Again he urged, "If the *halacha* agrees with me, let the walls of the house of study prove it!" The walls tilted as if to fall. But Rabbi Joshua rebuked the walls, saying, "When disciples of the wise are engaged in a halachic dispute, what right have you to interfere?" Hence, in deference to Rabbi Joshua they did not fall, and in deference to Rabbi Eliezer they did not resume their upright position; they are still standing at a slant.

Again Rabbi Eliezer said to the sages, "If the *halacha* agrees with me, let it be proved from heaven!"

A divine voice [literally, a *bat kol,* a divine voice that sounded like a young woman's voice] cried out, "Why do you dispute Rabbi Eliezer, with whom the *halacha* always agrees?" But Rabbi Joshua stood up and protested, "'The Torah is not in heaven'" (Deuteronomy 30:12). We pay no attention to a divine voice. . . ."

Rabbi Nathan met the prophet Elijah and asked him, "What did the Holy One do in that moment?"

"God laughed with joy, saying, 'My sons have defeated Me, My sons have defeated Me.'"

Here, sages are arguing about a piece of Jewish law. Rabbi Eliezer enlists a number of "tricks" to prove that he is correct. His colleagues will not accept it. Finally he appeals to a divine voice—only to be rebuffed by the biblical statement that "the Torah is not in heaven." Ever since revelation has stopped, ever since the Torah's completion, the sages no longer pay attention to divine voices. The truth of Jewish law can only be adduced through intellectual reasoning and the dialectic discussion of learned disciples.

The long-dead biblical prophet Elijah, who knows what is happening in the supernal realms, enters the conversation. Even though the divine voice was rejected, Elijah reports that God actually enjoyed the debate. As the modern Orthodox rabbi David Hartman wrote in *A Living Covenant*, post-biblical, Talmudic thinking liberates the intellect. God expresses self-limiting love for human beings by entrusting the elaboration of the Torah to rabbinic scholars.

God loved that the scholars were figuring things out for themselves—even if it meant that God "lost." For God that defeat was delightful. It is like the parent who loves being beaten in chess or in football by his or her child—or who loves it when his or her child comes back with a witty retort. God loves the fact that we are growing up, and no longer rely on the intervention of a Heavenly Parent. It's like when the father yells at his fighting children, "Go figure it out for yourselves!"

GOD WEEPS

God has frustrations and weeps—like a human father.

> God said: "So long as I am within the Holy Temple, the peoples of the world will be unable to touch it. However, I will shut My eyes and swear that I will have nothing to do with it again till the messianic end of time. Meanwhile, let

the enemies [the Romans] come and devastate it." At once the Romans entered the Temple and burned it. After it was burned, the Holy One said: "I have no dwelling place in the Land of Israel. So I shall remove My Presence from it and go up to My former residence [the heavens]."

God wept and said: "Woe is Me! For Israel's sake I caused My Presence to dwell below. But now that Israel sinned and I am returning to My former place, I have, Heaven forbid, become the laughingstock of the nations and an object of derision for mortals."

In that instant, the angel Metatron came, fell upon his face, and spoke before the Holy One: "Master of the universe, let me weep, but You must not weep." God replied: "If you do not let Me weep, I will go into a place where you have no authority to enter and weep there" (*Lamentations Rabbah,* 24).

Why must God not weep? After all, what would people say? A vulnerable God is so much at odds with our usual sense of God's omnipotence. But the rabbis were able to create the image of a vulnerable God because it suited their own self-image after the destruction of the Temple and Judean independence. Facing monumental loss, they were also vulnerable; they made God in their image.

SNAG (A SENSITIVE NEW AGE GOD)

Mature manhood is a combination of both masculine and feminine traits. Perhaps God is also a combination of those traits. The idea is not so strange. Moses embodies such a combination. In Numbers 11:12, Moses is burnt out from his ceaseless and thankless leadership role: "Did I conceive [or, "did I become pregnant"] with all this people? Did I give birth to them? Yet You say to me that I must carry them in my bosom as a nursing father [*omen*, like *emunah*, "faith"] carries an infant?"

Moses is not just teacher and leader. Moses is a mother as well. Moses' quasi-maternal role becomes the classic model of Torah teachers. Medieval Jewish pedagogical guides counsel that children be placed into the laps or bosoms of their teachers—in direct fulfillment of the above Biblical verse. As Ivan Marcus writes in *Rituals of Childhood: Jewish Acculturation in Medieval Europe*, the child leaves his natural mother at home and enters the culture of a new symbolic mother—a male Torah teacher!—who is now the model of a nurturing mother. In fact, an illustration in one medieval prayerbook portrays a male teacher holding a child on his lap in imitation of Madonna and Child! So, too, with God. God is a nurturing parent. As it turns out, God is not even a biological parent! God is an adoptive parent. This is good. It removes any notion of birth giving from a (male) god. More than that, it utterly divorces God's choice of Israel from the natural realm of things, making it supernatural and external to the normal patterns of history, making that selection even more remarkable.

Deuteronomy 32:10 ff. imagines Israel as a foundling child, and God as the One Who found that child

> in a desert region, in an empty howling waste. He engirded him, watched over him . . . like an eagle who rouses his nestlings, gliding down to his young. So did He spread His wings and take him, bear him along on His pinions. . . . He suckled him honey from the crag, and oil from the flinty rock.

The feminist thinker Rachel Adler finds this to be a striking example of the morphing of images of divinity. God's image moves from adoptive father to maternal eagle (who places her young birds on her wings, so that they would be protected from the bows of earthly hunters) to a mother who miraculously nurses out of the wastes of the desert.

More than that: A rabbinic legend (*Exodus Rabbah* 23:8) teaches that God ran a day-care center in Egypt for lost Israelite children!

When did the Holy One, Blessed Be He, cause the population of Israelites to grow so dramatically in Egypt? Exactly how did this happen?

When Pharaoh decreed: "Every male child shall be thrown into the Nile," what did the Israelite women do?

When a woman would sense that she was beginning to go into labor, she would go into the field to have the child.

Once the child was born, the mother would turn her eyes to heaven and say: "I have done my part, just as You told me—'Be fruitful and multiply'—Now You do *Your* part!"

And what did the Egyptians do? When the Egyptians saw the Israelite women going into the fields to have their children, they would sit opposite them at a distance.

When the women would finish delivering their children, and would return to the city, the Egyptians then took stones and went to kill the babies.

The babies would be swallowed up in the field, and then reappear at a distance, and again be swallowed up, and again reappear at a distance.

Finally, the Egyptians became weary of this and went away.

And how did the babies survive out in the fields?

There were some who said that the angels took care of the Israelite children. But others disagreed. Rabbi Chiyya the

Great said: God Himself would wash and clothe the children. He would feed them and He would clean them.

And the babies continued to grow in the field like the plants, and they would sneak into their houses mixed in with the flocks of sheep. . . .

But how did they know to go to their own parents?

The Holy One blessed be He would go with them, and show each one his parents' house, and God would say, "Call your father by this name, and your mother by this name."

The child would then say to the mother:

"Don't you remember when you bore me in a certain field on a certain day five months ago?"

And the mother would say: "Who raised you?"

And the child would say: "A certain young man, with nice curly hair. There is no one like him—and he is standing right outside the door."

They would go to look for him, but they could not find him.

And then, when they arrived at the Red Sea, and saw Him, the children would point Him out to their mothers and they would say:

"This is my God. This is the One who raised me in the fields."

The story is not to be believed. It is to be pondered. It reveals the deepest truth that we know about God. God is intimately involved in human history. The midrash imagines the Israelite mothers turning to God and saying: "We have done our parts . . . now You do *Your* part." Both parenting and the survival of the Jewish people result from the partnership between the divine and the human. The midrash imagines that it is God Who leads the Israelite children back to the houses of their parents. When we remember our parents' houses it is because God has led us there. The midrash imagines that the Israelite children saw God at the crossing of the Sea and sang out: "This is my God!" At the moment of freedom, we feel the very presence of God. Beyond the beautiful fable of God caring for the Israelite foundlings in Egypt, we hear the message that there is something in the universe very deep that cares for us with overwhelming passion and love. The midrash is trying to teach us that God cares passionately for the pain and suffering of humanity.

There is far more in the Jewish imagination than we know. We simply have not used it. When we do so, we become better, richer, deeper people—and men can become better, richer, deeper men as well. As Rabbi Henry Slonimsky, a prominent Reform thinker, once wrote, "Whatever else He may be, God is primarily and pre-eminently a great heart, caring most for what seems to be important and sacred to us, namely, our loves and aspirations and sufferings."

Men can be that great heart as well. That is what God wants—for us to bring that heart down to earth and to embody it.

INTRODUCTION

5: "In the City of Slaughter." From David Roskies, *The Literature of Destruction* (Philadelphia: Jewish Publication Society, 1989), 160–68.

CHAPTER ONE

16: "The Cain complex..." Yosef Hayim Yerushalmi, *Freud's Moses: Judaism Terminable and Interminable* (New Haven: Yale University Press, 1991), 92.

CHAPTER TWO

29: "Ishmael resembles Isaac..." Norman J. Cohen, *Self, Struggle, and Change* (Woodstock, Vt.: Jewish Lights Publishing, 1994), 71–72.

35: The connection of Esau with the Hebrew term *asah*. Rashi on Genesis 25:26.

42: "Isaac went there hoping to find Ishmael." Cohen, 89–90.

CHAPTER THREE

64: "As the late Professor Norman Mirsky noted..." See "Yavneh vs. Masada," in Mirsky, *Unorthodox Judaism* (Columbus: Ohio State University Press, 1978), 151–72.

66: "As the Zionist leader Berl Katznelson would write . . ." Quoted in Zerubavel, *Recovered Roots: Collective Memory and the Making of Israeli National Tradition* (Chicago: University of Chicago Press, 1995), 24.

CHAPTER FOUR

74: "As the late historian George Mosse has written, to duel meant having the same social status as your adversary." George Mosse, *The Image of Man: The Creation of Modern Masculinity* (New York: Oxford University Press, 1996), 19.

74: "In the City of Slaughter . . ." See Roskies, 160–68.

76: "The new Jews were to be 'deep-chested, sturdy, sharp-eyed Jews.'" Nordau, "Degeneration," quoted in Paul Breines, *Tough Jews: Political Fantasies and the Moral Dilemma of American Jewry* (New York: Basic Books, 1990), 144.

"As historian David Biale noted, the early Zionist congresses published postcards . . ." David Biale, *Eros and the Jews: From Biblical Israel to Contemporary America* (New York: Basic Books, 1992), 179.

79: "The great Israeli poet Uri Zvi Greenberg would write of 'masculinity rising in the climate of the land of the prophets . . .'" Uri Zvi Greenberg, *"Ha-Gavrut ha-Olah"* ("Masculinity Rising"), published in Tel Aviv in 1926. I am grateful to Professor Stanley Nash of Hebrew Union College–Jewish Institute of Religion for this reference.

82: "As Tom Segev wrote in his penetrating book *The Seventh Million: The Israelis and the Holocaust*, the Zionist goal was to create a new Jewish personality . . ." Tom Segev, *The Seventh Million: The Israelis and the Holocaust*, trans. Haim Watzman (New York: Hill and Wang, 1993), 169.

CHAPTER FIVE

96: Aryeh Lev Stollman, *The Far Euphrates* (New York: Riverhead Books, 1997), 191–93.

CHAPTER SIX

111: "It is an accepted view that we have to treat a man who beats his wife more severely..." From Joseph Karo's commentary on the *Shulchan Aruch, Bet Yosef, Even Ha-Ezer* 154:15.

CHAPTER SEVEN

139: "America forced men to measure their masculinity by being a breadwinner and by ascending to the middle class." Aviva Cantor, *Jewish Women, Jewish Men* (New York: HarperCollins, 1995), 170.

139: "As writer Tom Wolfe would put it, a 'social X-ray.'" See Tom Wolfe, *Bonfire of the Vanities* (New York: Farrar Straus and Giroux, 1987).

140: "In *The Time Bind*, Arlie Russell Hochschild..." cf. Arlie Russell Hochschild, *The Time Bind: When Work Becomes Home and Home Becomes Work* (New York: Metropolitan Books, 1997).

148: "According to Jewish mystical sources, Satan is drawn to holy acts, from which he derives nourishment." Quoted in Chava Weissler, *Voices of the Matriarchs: Listening to the Prayers of Early Modern Jewish Women* (Boston: Beacon Press, 1998), 109.

151: Stollman, *The Far Euphrates*, 163.

158: "Rabbi Yehude Leib Alter of Ger, the author of the Hasidic commentary *Sefat Emet*..." Arthur Green, *The Language of Truth* (Philadelphia: Jewish Publication Society, 1998), 37.

CHAPTER EIGHT

164: "In her book *Banished Knowledge*..." Alice Miller, *Banished Knowledge: Facing Childhood Injuries*, trans. Leila Vennewitz (New York: Doubleday, 1990), 139–40. The material on anti-circumcision groups is found in Mary Benedek, "Debate over Common American

Practice of Circumcision Reviewed," *New York Times*, May 19, 1996, IV; 3:1.

173: "As René Girard wrote in *Violence and the Sacred* (1986) . . ." Quoted in Tom F. Driver, *The Magic of Ritual: Our Need for Liberating Rites That Transform Our Lives and Our Communities* (New York: HarperCollins, 1991), 103.

176: "As novelist Philip Roth wrote in *The Counterlife* . . ." Philip Roth, *The Counterlife* (New York: Farrar Straus and Giroux, 1986), 323–24.

CHAPTER NINE

184: Abraham breaks the idols. This version of the legend in found in Hayim Nahman Bialik and Yehoshua Hana Ravitsky, eds., *The Book of Legends–Sefer Ha-Aggadah: Legends from the Talmud and Midrash*, trans. William G. Braude (New York: Schocken Books, 1992), 32.

189: "As Robert Bly writes . . ." Robert Bly, *Iron John: A Book About Men* (New York: Addison-Wesley, 1990), 16.

CHAPTER TEN

215: "As the Christian feminist Mary Daly wrote in *Beyond God the Father* . . ." Mary Daly, *Beyond God the Father: Toward a Philosophy of Women's Liberation* (Boston: Beacon Press, 1973), 13.

bibliography

Adler, Rachel. *Engendering Judaism: An Inclusive Theology and Ethics*. Philadelphia: Jewish Publication Society, 1998.

Biale, David. *Eros and the Jews: From Biblical Israel to Contemporary America*. New York: Basic Books, 1992.

Bialik, Hayim Nahman, and Yehoshua Hana Ravnitzky, eds. *The Book of Legends—Sefer Ha-Aggadah: Legends from the Talmud and Midrash*. Trans. William G. Braude. New York: Schocken Books, 1992.

Bly, Robert. *Iron John: A Book About Men*. New York: Addison-Wesley, 1990.

Boyarin, Daniel. *Carnal Israel: Reading Sex in Talmudic Culture*. Berkeley: University of California Press, 1993.

————. *Unheroic Conduct: The Rise of Heterosexuality and the Invention of the Jewish Man*. Berkeley: University of California Press, 1997.

Breines, Paul. *Tough Jews: Political Fantasies and the Moral Dilemma of American Jewry*. New York: Basic Books, 1990.

Bristow, Edward J. *Prostitution and Prejudice: The Jewish Fight Against White Slavery, 1870–1939*. New York: Schocken Books, 1983.

Brod, Harry. *A Mensch Among Men*. Fremont, Calif.: The Crossing Press, 1988.

Cantor, Aviva. *Jewish Women, Jewish Men: The Legacy of Patriarchy in Jewish Life*. New York: HarperCollins, 1995.

Cohen, Norman J. *Self, Struggle and Change: Family Conflict Stories in Genesis and Their Healing Insights for Our Lives*. Woodstock, Vt.: Jewish Lights Publishing, 1994.

Daly, Mary. *Beyond God the Father: Toward a Philosophy of Women's Liberation*. Boston: Beacon Press, 1973.

Frymer-Kensky, Tikva. *In the Wake of the Goddesses: Women, Culture, and the Biblical Transformation of Pagan Myth*. New York: Free Press, 1992.

Gilman, Sander L. *The Jew's Body*. New York: Routledge, 1991.

———. *Love + Marriage = Death and Other Essays on Representing Difference*. Stanford, Calif.: Stanford University Press, 1998.

———. *Smart Jews: The Construction of the Image of Jewish Superior Intelligence*. Lincoln: University of Nebraska Press, 1996.

Ginzberg, Louis. *The Legends of the Jews*. Philadelphia: Jewish Publication Society, 1925.

Gold, Michael. *Does God Belong in the Bedroom?* Philadelphia: Jewish Publication Society, 1992.

Green, Arthur, trans. *The Language of Truth: The Torah Commentary of the Sefat Emet, Rabbi Yehudah Leib Alter of Ger*. Philadelphia: Jewish Publication Society, 1998.

Gurian, Michael. *A Fine Young Man: What Parents, Mentors and Educators Can Do to Shape Adolescent Boys into Exceptional Men*. New York: Putnam, 1998.

Hirsh, Marilyn. *Captain Jiri and Rabbi Jacob*. New York: Holiday House, 1976.

Hoffman, Lawrence A. *Covenant of Blood: Circumcision and Gender in Rabbinic Judaism*. Chicago: University of Chicago Press, 1996.

Kugel, James. *The Bible as It Was*. Cambridge, Mass.: Harvard University Press, 1998.

Marcus, Ivan G. *Rituals of Childhood: Jewish Acculturation in Medieval Europe*. New Haven: Yale University Press, 1996.

Mirsky, Norman B. *Unorthodox Judaism*. Columbus: Ohio State University Press, 1978.

Mosse, George. *The Image of Man: The Creation of Modern Masculinity*. New York: Oxford University Press, 1996.

Neusner, Jacob. *Androgynous Judaism: Masculine and Feminine in the Dual Torah*. Macon, Ga.: Mercer University Press, 1993.

———. *The Enchantments of Judaism*. New York: Basic Books, 1987.

Pitzele, Peter. *Our Fathers' Wells: A Personal Encounter with the Myths of Genesis*. San Francisco: HarperSanFrancisco, 1995.

Plaskow, Judith. *Standing Again at Sinai: Judaism from a Feminist Perspective*. San Francisco: HarperSanFrancisco, 1991.

Raphael, Ray. *The Men from the Boys: Rites of Passage in Male America*. Lincoln: University of Nebraska Press, 1988.

Roskies, David. *The Literature of Destruction*. Philadelphia: Jewish Publication Society, 1989.

Rudavsky, T. M., ed. *Gender and Judaism: The Transformation of Tradition*. New York: New York University Press, 1995.

Schwartz, Regina. *The Curse of Cain: The Violent Legacy of Monotheism*. Chicago: University of Chicago Press, 1997.

Segev, Tom. *The Seventh Million: The Israelis and the Holocaust*. Translated by Haim Watzman. New York: Hill and Wang, 1993.

Seidman, Naomi. *A Marriage Made in Heaven: The Sexual Politics of Hebrew and Yiddish*. Berkeley: University of California Press, 1997.

Soloveitchik, Joseph B. *The Lonely Man of Faith*. New York: Doubleday, 1992.

Stollman, Aryeh Lev. *The Far Euphrates*. New York: Riverhead Books, 1997.

Yerushalmi, Yosef Hayim. *Freud's Moses: Judaism Terminable and Interminable*. New Haven: Yale University Press, 1991.

Zerubavel, Yael. *Recovered Roots: Collective Memory and the Making of Israeli National Tradition.* Chicago: University of Chicago Press, 1995.

Zornberg, Aviva Gottlieb. *Genesis: The Beginning of Desire.* Philadelphia: Jewish Publication Society, 1995.

index